AN INTRODUCTION TO

QUANTITATIVE RESEARCH METHODS

FOR LIBRARIANS

2nd Edition
Revised

by

Taverekere Srikantaiah, Ph.D.

Systems Specialist
World Bank

and

Herbert H. Hoffman

Catalog Librarian
Santa Ana College

1978

HEADWAY PUBLICATIONS

Suggested cataloging:

Srikantaiah, Taverekere
   An introduction to quantitative research
methods for librarians. 2d ed. By Taverekere Srikantaiah and Herbert H. Hoffman.
Santa Ana, California, Headway Publications,
1977.

   1. LIBRARY EDUCATION. 2. LIBRARY
SCIENCE--RESEARCH. I. Hoffman, Herbert
H., jt. auth. II. Title: Quantitative research
methods for librarians. III. Title.

Z 669.8 S7   020.72

ISBN 0-89537-002-6

DEDICATED WITH AFFECTION TO
OUR LOVING WIVES,
Jayashree Srikantaiah
Rita Hoffman

ACKNOWLEDGEMENTS

This work could not have been completed without the encouragement of Mrs. Doris Banks, Director of the Division of Library Science, California State University, Fullerton. She took personal interest in our efforts and helped us in many ways.

We are also thankful to our colleagues in the Division and to Bhodan S. Wynar and the staff of Libraries Unlimited, Inc., of Littleton, Colorado, for their valuable comments and contributions which helped us sharpen our concepts, correct errors, and refine our presentation.

Sincere thanks are also extended to the Division's office staff, especially Mrs. Norma Morris and Mrs. Flora McNall, for their time and energy, and to Miss Terry Spaise who did an excellent job of typing the original manuscript.

PREFACE

We believe that library science is a field with problems similar in complexity to those of many other fields, from business to sociology. Modern investigations of library phenomena have taken on an increasingly rigorous and quantitative hue. Circulation data are evaluated by means of statistical models. Library holdings data are considered in terms of probability distributions. Confidence levels for sample studies have become de rigeur. Correlation coefficients are standard indicators of relationships. Data analysis, not description, is emphasised in library research today.

Consequently, quantitative research methodology, foreign to the curriculum of most library schools a decade ago, is becoming standard fare. While teaching such a mandatory course in research methodology in the Division of Library Science, California State University, Fullerton, we found that there are many good books on the subject, but no American work that addresses itself specifically to the problems of library science. We have attempted here a narrative, non-mathematical approach to research methodology, stressing logic and the reasoning underlying what we conceive of as the basic methods of quantitative research. We have also taken care to draw our examples strictly from the library field.

Taverekere Srikantaiah
Herbert H. Hoffman

TABLE OF CONTENTS

INTRODUCTION:
WHY QUANTITATIVE
LIBRARY RESEARCH?

To many people "library research" means looking for bibliographic information, searching the card catalog, or using the Readers Guide to Periodical Literature. This, of course, is not what is meant in the present context by the term "library research". What the authors are concerned with in this book are ways to conduct investigations into the myriad problems that arise in connection with the institution, selection, operation, optimization, estimation, justification, and evaluation of library services, and with the explanation, generalization, and prediction of library phenomena of all kinds.

Examples of such phenomena discussed in library science journals in recent months included problems of dividing the card catalog, of determining the least-used materials in a library, of forecasting library growth in the face of changing economic conditions, of acquisitions overkill, of open vs. closed shelves, of shortening or lengthening loan periods, of the influence of non-print media on the accustomed patterns of bibliographic organization and control, and many more.

These problems are real and answers must be found. Undoubtedly, librarianship faces a stepped up program of research in the years to come. Librarians who would conduct meaningful research must be cognizant of relevant research methodology. Few will deny, therefore, that the development of skill in the conduct of research is a necessary part of a librarian's education. But why, the reader may ask, should there be emphasis on quantitative research methods?

The answer is simple. Unless research is based on data that can be quantified it carries little or no weight. Non-quantitative or subjective research techniques are characterized by emphasis on human experience and judgement. There are few if any data involved. Such research typically begins with assumptions, with conditions that "stand to reason", with things that are common knowledge. People's opinions are the primary inputs. The results rest on authority and belief more than on evidence.

Here is an example. Two years ago, the dictionary catalog of a Western university library was converted into a three-way divided catalog. One of the reasons given for this change was stated thus: "It was _thought_ that the three catalogs would provide ... decreased congestion" (italics ours). The reader should notice that the project rested on a simple, subjective judgement: it was thought (assumed? hoped?) that it would work. There was no factual basis for the decision, a typical flaw of the non-quantitative approach to research.

The methods of quantitative or objective research, on the other hand, are characterized by reliance on observable, measurable data. The results are exact. In terms of the data, which are open for inspection, confidence can be stated with precision. Here is an example from the field. Two years ago a Midwestern university library reported a change in loan policy from semester loans to four-week loans. The decision to shorten the loan period, like the Western university's decision to divide the catalog, was based on expected benefits. But the expectations, in this case, were reached with the aid of a previously tested mathematical model. This model involved certain probability distributions as well as numerical statements of different loan policies. When the quantified policies were systematically changed during a computer simulation run, an optimum loan period was computed. This is the loan period that the library adopted. Subsequent monitoring of circulation activities showed a marked improvement in the availability of books, as predicted by the simulation.

It is the authors' contention that all serious library research of the future will be quantitative in nature. We believe that change in library operations or services will increasingly have to be justified by clearly demonstrable benefits, not in terms of "shoulds" or impassioned statements of opinion but in terms of cold numbers, particularly numbers of dollars. Personal judgement expressed in words will not be taken much longer as evidence of progress in library science. Whether people say they like their library or not, for example, will become irrelevant. What will count will be the number of people using the facility. The design of the QUIET sign will be unimportant. What counts will be the measured decibels in the reading room. That we have "always done it this way" will not be an acceptable argument. The only good library will be the one that fulfills its objectives!

Our point is that all serious library research must be based, ultimately, on criteria that are observed, counted, or measured. Quantitative library research, then, is not just one of many useful methods in the librarian's repertoire of problem solving systems. It is the very core, the essence, the sine qua non of all scientific inquiry into library phenomena.

1. THE GENERAL
RESEARCH DESIGN

Little in life is automatic. If a research project is to yield relevant answers it must be carefully designed to ask the right questions. It would be folly, for example, simply to begin questioning library patrons without having determined beforehand how to evaluate their responses. Obviously, one does not begin a research project by observing just anything. One must first establish what it is one wants to know. A study of reading room sound level preferences of library users will not profit from a count of people sitting at individual carrels unless a relationship between carrel location and sound level has first been established. In other words, the collection of data cannot yield the desired answers unless the questions are well directed. The questions, in turn, cannot be well directed if the problem is not clear, and so on. In the planning of any research project, therefore, the detailed and systematic design of all steps to be undertaken is of the greatest importance.

Just how many steps there are in a proper research design is a matter of personal judgement. No absolute dogma can be laid down. But the vital steps can be enumerated. Figure 1 shows a comprehensive schematic of the major steps in a research design. There are eleven boxes in this schematic. These boxes represent the major steps. No serious study, for example, can be conducted without some sort of a theoretical foundation. The more solid the theory, the sharper will be the focus of the research. This is why the question of theoretical guidelines is introduced at the very top of the schematic.

Research, as will be shown later, can be conducted on a very simple fact finding or survey level (in answer to the question: who is?) as well as on the higher plane of finding the causes of phenomena (in answer to the question: why is it?). As the schematic of figure 1 shows, the different levels of research require different procedures of data evaluation. Box 1 represents this division into two types of research.

(3)

4

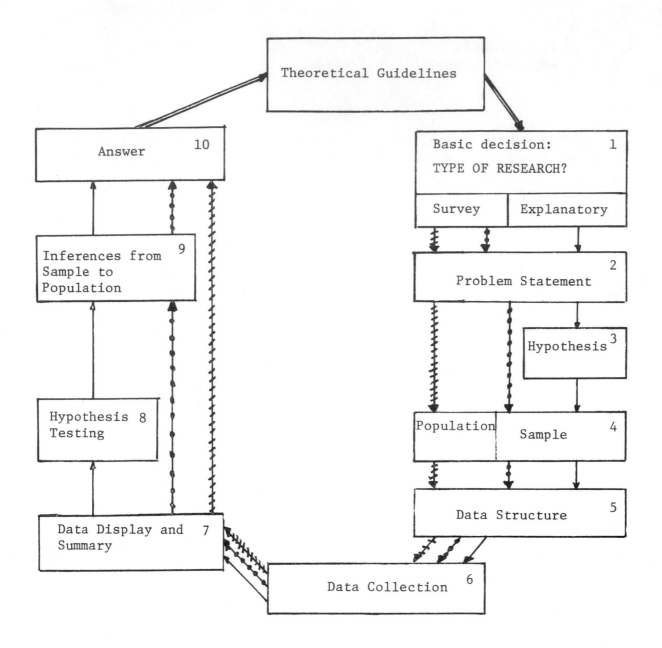

Figure 1. Comprehensive schematic of the
major steps in a research design

——————— Explanatory research
•–•–•–•– Survey research based on sample
✝✝✝✝✝✝ Survey research based on population

Of course, regardless of type of research, no investigator can go far if the very research problem is not clear to him. It seems obvious that a problem statement (Box 2) must be part of any research design. If the study is to be an explanatory study one or more hypotheses (Box 3) must be formulated, for what else is scientific research if not the testing of hypotheses?

A research design must also include considerations of the population of people or objects studied, and of possible sampling methods (Box 4). Another important step is to recognize what sort of data will be needed to answer the questions asked and to test the hypotheses set up (Box 5). Depending on the nature of the data, decisions must be made early in the research design phase how to collect these data (Box 6).

No research design is complete unless arrangements are included for the summarization and display of the data (Box 7). All expanatory designs must include plans for the testing of hypotheses (Box 8). All sample studies must allow for inferences to the population (Box 9). Omit any of these major steps and you will not find the answer (Box 10).

The order of the steps in the general research design of figure 1 is not arbitrary or based on opinion or preferences. The steps are mandatory because of the nature of research. The person who wants to compute the gas mileage for his automobile must do certain things. He must keep a record of gasoline bought and of miles travelled (data collection!). He must then divide the gallons of fuel consumed into the miles travelled (data analysis!). If properly done, these steps will yield the answer. For the same reasons the librarian who would conduct a research project, a scientific investigation into library phenomena, must follow the guidelines given in figure 1. The importance of developing a good research design cannot be overemphasized. In fact, it can be said that by far the major part of the intellectual energy that goes into a research project is expended on the research design. However, once the design cycle for a proposed study has been completed the work is at least half done. Once the plan is ready the execution is reduced to a routine.

Naturally, the librarian who wants to evaluate a published research report will also do best to follow the same research design schematic. Suppose the problem statement of a published research report indicated that the object of the study was to discover the reason for a certain phenomenon. The skilled reader immediately classifies this as an explanatory research project and looks for a stated hypothesis. If none can be found the rest of the report must be discounted considerably for it cannot very well support or disprove a hypothesis that was never stated.

Likewise, if the report of an explanatory study contained detailed hypotheses, meticulous accounts of the data collection methods employed, elaborate tabulations of the data thus collected, but made no mention of the steps taken to analyse the data, the answers will not carry much weight because they are based on a weak design: hypotheses cannot be supported by descriptive statistics alone!

On the other hand, a report that clearly indicates the problem, states the hypotheses, makes clear that a sample was selected for the study, reveals the nature of the data and the collection methods, displays and summarizes the data conveniently, and then elaborates on the statistical tests employed to support or disprove the stated hypotheses will yield answers that are confidence inspiring if only because of the flawless elegance of the methodology. Such a report, following the steps outlined in figure 1, can be considered a good report. The reader can concentrate on the implications of the research without misgivings.

Since the research design cycle from problem statement to answer is the alpha and the omega of all scientific research the rest of this book can be considered a box-by-box elaboration on the schematic of figure 1.

2.   THEORETICAL
        GUIDELINES

There are many definitions of "theory". Some say a theory is the
same as a model: an analogy, not precise and certainly not all-explaining.
Others will prefer a broader definition: a theory is a systematic account
of some field of study, derived from a set of general propositions.

In the context of research methodology in library science we offer this
comprehensive definition: a theory is a set of coherent, empirically or
experientially substantiated constructs that explain library phenomena.
We might add that such constructs grow out of hypotheses and are usually
in the process of modification or further substantiation.

As we said before, and will have to say again, no research is possible
without a theoretical foundation. Let us demonstrate the importance of
theoretical guidelines in library research by means of an example from
the field. Suppose a librarian had discovered that library users often fail
to find their information in the library. The problem involves the process
by which a user finds his information sources through the catalog.
Instinctively, a researcher faced with a problem wants to gather facts as
the next step in his investigation. But must he not first take time to
determine what he needs to know, what facts to gather? Suppose the
investigator working on the catalog failure problem went out and asked
everybody "what do you think of the card catalog?" Here are some
probable answers: "it is o.k."; "I don't know"; "great!". He probably
would not know what to do with such vague answers to a general, aimless
question.

To give direction to one's research he needs to theorize first. If a
theoretical explanation or solution to the problem can be found the
investigator will know what data to collect. The hypothetical researcher
interested in the reasons for user failure at the catalog might theorize
that there is a relationship between the way the literature is structured
and the way the catalog is constructed, and also between the way the user
approaches the catalog and the way it is organized. These relationships
can be visualized by means of a drawing:

(7)

8

Information
seeker's   Catalog
search pattern   organization

Information
source
structure

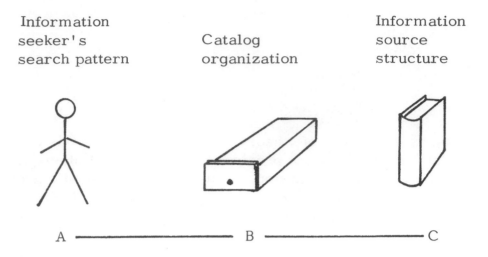

A ——————————— B ——————————— C

Figure 2. User-Library relationships

The drawing shows how an information seeker uses the card catalog to find his information source. There are two relationships involved. On the left side (A -- B) is the seeker's search pattern and how that is related to the catalog. On the right side (B -- C) is the relationship between the structure of the media and the organization of the catalog.

First, consider the relationship between C and B. How does the structure of the literature influence the organization of the catalog? To get to the bottom of this question one must first determine what, theoretically, "C" and "B" look like.

In a well developed field of science theoretical frameworks exist, constructs, classifications, that serve to provide the basis for further work.

Library science has been characterized as an empirical science, a field of knowledge based on traditional practice and chance experience rather than on systematic research. Inevitably, this picture is changing. As more and more phenomena of the library world become the subject of investigations librarians begin to identify and develop the theoretical foundations underlying their practices. What theoretical frameworks do librarians have to work with in respect to the structure of documents and catalogs? One possible construct is the work/book/set theory of the structure of information sources developed by Hoffman.[1] In its first part, the work/book relationship, this

---

1. Descriptive Cataloging in a New Light: Polemical chapters for Librarians, by Herbert H. Hoffman. Santa Ana, CA, Headway Publications, 1976. Ch.1.

theory states that all documents, regardless of medium, consist of works (intellectual units) packaged in books (containers). Consider a play of 54 pages. It is some playwright's intellectual effort, a work. But is it a book? It could be. If some publisher packaged this play alone between boards he could call the resulting publication a book. Chances are the play will find itself in the company of ten others, all included in one volume. Clearly the play is not a book in this case. The entire collection is a book.

Immediately it becomes clear that structurally speaking a book is a physical entity, a packaging unit, that contains one or more intellectual units or works. The distinction between book and work is the distinction between container and contents. It is a very important distinction for catalog organization and information searching alike. For by means of the relationship between works and books it can be shown that books are of several types -- there are single work, single volume books, for example, but also multiple work, single volume books, to mention only two types -- and that catalogs, too, are of several types. There are at one extreme catalogs that are entirely dedicated to the recording of books, containers. They contain no work analytics. There are probably very few of these. And at the other extreme one can conceive of a catalog that is completely analytical. It provides an entry for every single work in the collection, for every poem, every story, every play. There probably are not any in real life. Real, existing card catalogs are partially analytic. They can be positioned on the book side of the continuum, perhaps in position R in the following diagram:

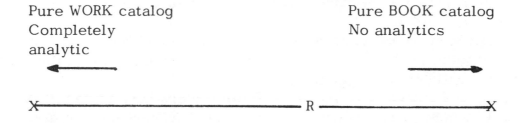

Pure WORK catalog   Pure BOOK catalog
Completely   No analytics
analytic

X————————————————R————————————X

The concept of the work/book relationship provides a theoretical framework for the study of catalog use for it can now be shown that users of libraries are primarily people looking for plays, novels, stories, treatises, articles. In other words, library users are work seekers. If it can be established by careful questioning that this is indeed so a theoretical explanation emerges for the fact that some users are not successful at the card catalog: they may be work seekers using a predominantly book oriented catalog. They look for the titles of intellectual units in a catalog that lists only the titles of containers. This theoretical explanation, the reader will recognize, leads directly to a hypothesis that can be tested.

Diligent and careful questioning of users can now be focussed on precise, relevant questions such as "are you looking for a book that contains one single work?" instead of general, irrelevant ones such as "how do you feel about the catalog?". If the answers show that users are mostly looking for smaller works contained in collections this would explain frequent user failure at the catalog. It would put the blame on the catalog. Corrective action could then be taken, such as more analytical added entries or better guiding to published indexes.

If, on the other hand, the answers show that users search the catalog primarily for works that are published as independent units (single work, one volume books) a different explanation must be found by further probing and questioning. Here are some other possible causes for lack of user success:

> Library's fault
> > a poor collection (library does not have what user needs)
> > a poor catalog (slow or improper cataloging)

> User's fault
> > lack of bibliographic sophistication (does not understand
> > > structure of literature)
> > lack of library knowledge (does not understand filing rules)

Each of these and many more tentative explanations can now be tested. If enough possible solutions are tested the true cause of user failure at the card catalog will eventually be uncovered.

Regardless of the objective of research similar steps have to be followed in all cases. Ultimately, it is always the theoretical framework that gives the essential direction to an investigation. Without this direction one should simply not know what to look for, what data to collect. Research efforts undertaken without the benefit of a theoretical basis, not uncommon in the library literature of the past, lead to the paradoxical situation of answers to which there are no questions!

3.　TYPES OF
　　RESEARCH

Research, including quantitative research, is not all of one kind. It can
be conducted on several levels. One can visualize the research process as
a continuum extending from simple fact finding at one end to the discovery
of causes of phenomena at the other end. Here is a graphical representation
of this continuum, showing several intermediate levels:

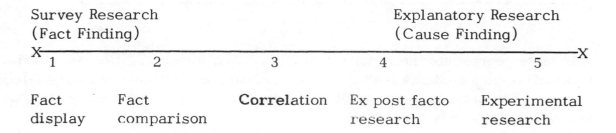

Survey research is characterized by an emphasis on data collection and
the subsequent intuitive evaluation or simple comparison of the displayed
findings. The researcher stands apart and looks, as it were, at the data to
see _what_ there is. This type of research can also be called "fact finding"
research. Fact finding research is shown at the left end of the continuum.
　　At the other end is explanatory research. This is characterized by an
emphasis on data analysis and the explanation of phenomena. The researcher
is not so much interested in seeing what there is but in _why_ it is there. This
type of research can also be called "cause finding" research.
　　The continuum line has been marked in five places. The left-most mark,
1, stands for fact display. This is the simplest level on which research can be
conducted. The investigator finds what the facts are. Here is an example.
Some time ago, Robert Sommer published a brief report on a study concerned
with the adequacy of reading areas in college libraries as study places. His
problem situation was the lack of information on how users feel about the

lighting, noise level, and ventilation in a library. Sommer therefore began his report by stating the problem: "How do readers feel about the lighting, the noise level, and the ventilation?". The answers obtained from a sample of readers might well have been in terms of ratings. Here is a (fictitious) display:

	Number of Reader Ratings				
	Excellent	Good	Fair	Poor	No opinion
Lighting	1000	990	350	1	10
Noise	900	900	800	200	9
Ventilation	1200	600	300	20	20

This table represents the results of a fact finding mission. It gives a certain measure of how students feel about the reading room climate of their college library. The project is purely descriptive, however. It does not explain why students feel the way they do.

The next point on the continuum, 2, stands for fact comparisons. Here, too, the investigator finds the facts. A typical problem might be stated like this: how does the budget of library X compare with that of library Y? After studying the finances of the two libraries a researcher may be able to state that Library X's budget has been increasing over the years while the budget of Library Y has diminished. He then displays the findings in comparable form:

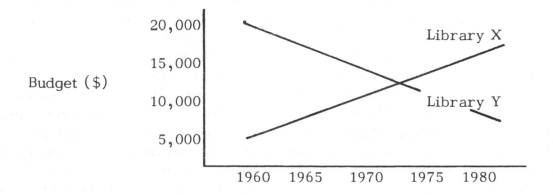

This is still descriptive research. It does not explain why the budgets went the way they did. But such comparative research is on a level that allows rudimentary evaluative conclusions to be drawn.

The middle point on the continuum, 3, stands for correlational studies. These also belong into the realm of descriptive research. Such studies involve two or more observations on each subject studied. The investigator studies the relationships of the data. A correlation between number of books read by college students, for example, and the grades obtained by these same students allows prediction: the more books a student reads the better grades he will obtain. This is research on a level considerably above simple descriptive studies. It requires the use of fairly involved mathematical procedures that will be discussed in chapter 9.

The last two points on the continuum, 4 and 5, stand for higher levels of explanatory research that cannot be described in simple terms here. Suffice it to say that ex post facto and experimental research go beyond data description. Such research is conducted to find the causes of previously unexplained or inadequately explained phenomena and involves statistical methods of data analysis. A detailed discussion of these methods begins with chapter 11.

It should be pointed out that the borderline between survey research and explanatory research is not sharp. The two types of research overlap considerably. A correlation study, for example, may be used to establish nothing more than that two variables are related. This is essentially a form of survey research. But a correlation study may also be the beginning of a study to show that one variable influences the other, an explanatory project.

4. PROBLEM STATEMENTS
AND HYPOTHESES

Survey   Research

    All survey research is research aimed at discovering the facts in a
problem situation. Since it is impossible to gather relevant facts unless
the problem is well understood survey research must always begin with a
carefully phrased problem statement. A good problem statement describes
the exact dimensions of a concrete, specific situation. One cannot
investigate a vague generality such as "library information transfer" per
se, for example. This may be a problem, but the statement is not precise
enough. It lacks measurable criteria and clear definitions. The definitions
in a problem statement may seem laborious at times. One writer found
that his problem involved, among other things, the construct "noise". He
offered this definition: "Whenever a message is sent there exists the
possibility that the received message will contain flaws ... the presence
of these disruptive factors is called noise -- factors which disrupt both
message transmission and message receiving by introducing distortions
into the system". Laborious or not, this definition leaves no doubt in the
reader's mind what kind of noise is meant.

    To arrive at precise definitions often requires considerable work.
Consider the question of reference desk location. As it stands, "location"
is an abstract construct that the mind cannot operate on. It must be
defined in such terms as "how many feet from the desk to the card
catalog?", a relatively simple definition of "location". But consider also
the problem of "architectural design". This is another abstract concept
that must be defined in operational, concrete terms. This means that it
must be analysed into observable criteria. Clearly, "architectural design"
as such cannot be observed. But some of its components can be observed.
An investigator can, for example, observe a building's capacity to shelter
occupants from outside light and temperature. He can observe the
placement of intercommunication channels such as doors, hallways, and
stairs. He can evaluate the effects of partitions, the comfort level of
furniture, and many more criteria. Only when the relevant components

(14)

of the concept "architectural design" have been precisely defined, when the concept has been operationalized, is it possible to collect the facts and study the "architectural design" of a building.

This process of sharpening a vaguely sensed difficulty (information transfer, location, architectural design) to one or more precise questions (noise or message distortion, distance in feet, capacity to shelter occupants from sunlight), questions that are at least conceptually capable of being answered, is the essence of good problem formulation in survey research.

Explanatory Research

In explanatory research the interest is in relationships between facts. To channel and guide one's data collection and data analysis efforts one must first establish what data are needed and how these can be analysed. This is done by means of a research hypothesis.

A hypothesis states a proposed solution or answer to a problem. Consider the problem of the divided catalog. Many libraries face this problem. The question is evaluative: is the divided catalog adequate? A measurable criterion must be established, perhaps user failure -- number of instances when a user failed to find a book because he mistook a title for a subject heading, or such. If this criterion is adopted the following hypothesis (proposed solution) emerges: "dividing the catalog will result in a reduction of instances of user failure".

This hypothesis is precisely worded. It is stated in operational terms, i.e. there are measurable criteria. It is testable: an investigator can experiment, collect data, and see if the expected reduction of user failure actually occurs.

A hypothesis is always sharp, specific, and quantified. It expresses magnitude in numbers. Terms such as "large" and "small" would not adequately describe quantitative measurements or observations. The problem in a research project may be to find out if large families prevent mothers from using the public library. The investigator could define "large family" as a family with three or more children. An unambiguous hypothesis can then be formulated like this: "Mothers with three or more children use the library significantly less often than childless women or mothers of one or two children".

General definitions ("the catalog is a finding tool") or sweeping generalizations ("libraries are important) must never be mistaken for hypotheses. Also, hypotheses contain a minimum of untested assumptions ("the library is the heart of the college" or "every library needs a card catalog"). Such assumptions are in the nature of a priori propositions, statements that are self evident. A priori assumptions "stand to reason" but not necessarily to experience, and that is why they have no place in research hypotheses.

All scientific research, including research into the causes of library phenomena, ultimately reduces to the testing of hypotheses, to the analysis of data in order to establish or rule out relationships between two or more variables. This is why a testable research hypothesis is a necessary step in _any_ explanatory research project, without exception. It is also a step that must precede the data collection step. While this last remark appears obvious, the importance of it has escaped many researchers in the past. How many questionnaires have been mailed out by librarians who had only the vaguest idea of what to do with the answers after they arrived!

5. POPULATIONS AND DATA

In discussing survey and explanatory research we must also consider the following distinctions. A researcher may be interested in one fact, observed on one single subject or unit (for example, one library). Possibly, however, a researcher may want to establish a fact that is generally true for the entire population or universe of observable units (for example, all libraries). In both cases, the researcher collects his data from all observable units. In technical terms, he takes a "census".

Often, of course, a census is out of the question. Who can interview, for example, "all" librarians? Researchers therefore usually settle for a compromise. They collect their data from a sample of the universe of observable units (for example, one hundred librarians). The results obtained from the sample are then extended to the entire population by means of statistical procedures allowing for sampling error.

Research, then, can be based on data collected from one single observation, from an entire population of subjects, or from a sample. Putting these different aspects together we obtain the following summary table:

	Fact finding A	Fact comparison B	Correlation C	Ex post facto D	Experiment E
1. Single observation (case study)	1A	1B			
2. Population (census)	2A	2B	2C		
3. Sample	3A	3B	3C	3D	3E

Fact Finding Research

If the reader studies the summary table he should notice that cell 1A represents the simplest possible fact finding research design. There is one single unit to be observed, perhaps one library. The investigator's question might be: "How large a staff has this library?". The answer might be: "Seven persons". Conceptually, this survey is the simplest research design, located at the lowest level on the continuum scale on page 11.

Compare that with cell 2A. Here we might consider a study of all the public libraries in Blank County, California. Perhaps there are twenty such libraries. We might amass the following information:

	Number of persons on staff
Library 1	7
Library 2	5
.	.
.	.
.	.
Library 20	8

At the end of the study we shall know precisely what size staff each and every public library in that county has. We might compute a summary statistic such as the mean staff size (How to do this will be discussed in chapter 8). We are then in a position to state the average, the population mean for the variable "staff size" in Blank County libraries. The data, of course, are nothing more than twenty head counts, a simple arithmetic operation relatively low on the continuum scale.

Now look at cell 3A. Here we are dealing with data based on a sample. Perhaps we are concerned with the population consisting of all single-branch public library systems in Zip Code area 9. There may be several hundred of these. Rather than conduct several hundred head counts to establish the mean population value of the variable "staff size"we might opt to settle for an estimate of that value. We draw a sample of one hundred libraries and conduct one hundred head counts. The resulting summary value represents an estimate of the true value. Here is a diagram to visualize the process:

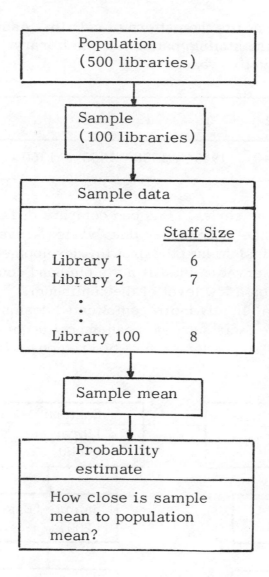

As the diagram reveals the design involves a little more than simple head counts. It requires a probability estimate. This is a question of statistical inference, a method that allows a researcher to estimate the closeness of the sample results to the truth. More of this in chapters 11 and 12. This design is on a slightly higher level on the continuum scale.

Fact Comparison Research

Now for a design that fits the pattern of cell 1B. Assume you wished to establish the history of the staffing pattern in one library. You might utilize data collected over thirty-five years:

Staff :	1	2	3	4	5	6	7	8
Year:	1935	1940	1945	1950	1955	1960	1965	1970

The data constitute a time series. One can compare different values of a variable such as "staff size", a quantity that "varies", over a certain stretch of time in order to gain insight into the growth, development, or history of a phenomenon. Each observation is still a simple head count, however, and this design therefore is on a low level of the continuum.

Cell 3B describes a slightly more complicated design. A researcher may wish to compare two facts such as mean annual acquisition budgets derived from two samples, one for each of two regions. Here is a diagram of the situation:

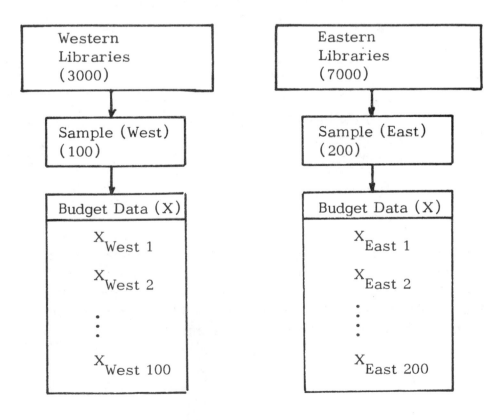

In addition to being a fact finding mission involving a budget figure for each of three hundred libraries this design also calls for statistical estimates of sampling error and possibly for an evaluation of the significance of the difference between two sets of data. It occupies a higher level on the continuum scale. Other aspects of this design will be discussed in chapters 14 and 15.

Correlation   Research

If cell 3B calls for two samples(two groups of libraries) each of which yields a value for one variable (annual budget), then cell 3C calls for one sample which yields values for two or more variables. Here is a diagram of such a situation:

```
                    ┌─────────────────────────┐
                    │  Population             │
                    │  (500 libraries)        │
                    └─────────────────────────┘
                              │
                    ┌──────────────────────┐
                    │  Sample              │
                    │  (100 libraries)     │
                    └──────────────────────┘
                              │
┌───────────────────────────────────────────────────────────────┐
│                                                                 │
│                     Variable X          Variable Y             │
│                     Acquisition         Staff size             │
│                     rate                                        │
│                     ────────            ─────────              │
│                                                                 │
│   Library 1            X₁                  Y₁                   │
│                                                                 │
│   Library 2            X₂                  Y₂                   │
│                                                                 │
│      ⋮                 ⋮                   ⋮                    │
│                                                                 │
│   Library 100          X₁₀₀               Y₁₀₀                 │
│                                                                 │
└───────────────────────────────────────────────────────────────┘
```

This is a typical correlation design. While the investigator has no control over any of the variables and is therefore compelled to simply observe "what is", correlation nevertheless requires sophisticated statistical procedures to establish the direction and strength of the presumed relationship between the variables X and Y. While still of the nature of fact finding research (is there a relationship, not

<u>what causes</u> the relationship!), this design is located fairly high on the continuum scale. The details of correlation will be discussed in chapter 9.

If we look at cell 3D we see that we have passed from survey research into the region of explanatory research. Such research is conducted to discover the cause of an event. It is therefore always concerned with the relationships between two or more variables. This is so because any event is the result of a change from one state of being to another. To be noticeable, this change must be observable as a variation in some criterion. A library may be empty in the morning, and crowded in the afternoon. Clearly, there is a change between morning and afternoon. The criterion variable "number of patrons in the library" shows variation. This variation is not spontaneous. It is the consequence of something else. Possibly the sun was shining in the morning, while it rained in the afternoon. In other words, there is a second variable, weather, which also changed. There is at least a suspicion that the change in the variable "weather" is the cause of the change in the variable "number of patrons in the library".

It is important to make the nature of such relationships between two variables very clear. By tradition, one of them is designated as the dependent variable, the other as the independent variable. A causal relationship is established when a change in the independent variable (weather) is followed or accompanied by a change in the dependent variable (number of patrons in the library). Explanatory research hinges upon whether or not it can be convincingly demonstrated that the change in the independent variable was the cause of the observed change in the dependent variable.

Ex post facto Research

There are two procedures to do this. Cell 3D in the table of page 17 points to a project in the region labelled Ex post facto Research. Such research is conducted to discover the causes of an event after this event has already happened. In the library field and in many other fields, particularly in the social sciences, one often has a wealth of data that represent observations of things that have already occurred. There is no possible way to go back and make them happen again. In other words, one cannot experiment.

A researcher might observe that poor people read fewer books than wealthier people. There would appear to be a causal relationship between wealth and reading activity. But to test this the researcher cannot expropriate a sample of wealthy people just to see if they will stop to read once they have become poor. The librarian must be satisfied with observations of the library habits of groups of people that belong to certain socio-economic groups. Much of what we know about library affairs is based on such observations of data "after they have happened" or, to use the customary Latin phrase, ex post facto research. The method is therefore of the greatest importance.

In ex post facto research one begins by observing the dependent variable, the effect (number of patrons in the library; reading habits of different people). One then searches backwards for possible causes. Unfortunately this is not as easy as it may sound. For there are many potential causes for any given phenomenon. The influx of patrons in the afternoon may be due to the rain. But it may also be due to prevailing school and office hours, to the lack of parking facilities in the busy morning hours, or to any number of other independent variables.

Since the investigator has no certain way to determine which of many possible factors is the true cause of the phenomenon under discussion he must use the method of agreement and difference, logical thinking patterns that go back to John Stuart Mill's "double method of agreement". Mill found that where a number of observed instances of a phenomenon under investigation have only one circumstance in common, while that circumstance is the only one absent when the phenomenon cannot be observed, then that circumstance can be assumed to be causally connected with the phenomenon under investigation. This difficult sentence does make good sense when it is carefully studied. But it also points to the major flaw of the ex post facto method. For the method requires that all possible rival conclusions be ruled out before one is finally selected. And because the number of possible contributing causes is unlimited it is impossible to arrive at a totally convincing conclusion via ex post facto research. If X is caused by D, but the investigator examines only A, B, and C he shall never discover the truth!

Experimental Research

Whenever possible, therefore, the researcher who seriously wants to get to the heart of a research problem will try to use an experimental design. To find the cause of a phenomenon through experimental research an investigator must set up laboratory conditions such that change can be introduced in an independent variable and the effect of that change observed on a dependent variable.

The simplest experimental design is the single case observation. Here is a schematic:

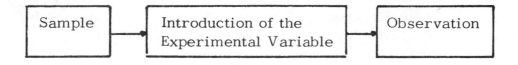

Unfortunately, the single case design provides no comparison data. If we were to open the doors of a new library on Monday morning after having sponsored a program on the local radio station the weekend before (an independent variable) and great throngs of people came the first day (the dependent variable we are interested in) we might wish to conclude that our pet idea, the radio program, caused the observed avalanche. In reality, of course, there is no proof whatsoever that the program had anything to do with the number of people present on opening day.

A slightly more sophisticated experimental design is the group comparison. Here is an example. Perhaps a problem has arisen in a certain library: the workload resulting from the processing of overdue notices has risen to an intolerable level. The librarian has a hunch that the reason people keep books overdue is not so much that they are mean or forgetful. They simply need more time to read the books they check out. The loan period in this hypothetical library is currently two weeks. If the librarian's hunch has merit it follows that the number of overdues should be reduced if the loan period is changed from two to four weeks.

Since this is a situation where the librarian is in a position to introduce variation in the independent variable "loan period" while leaving everything else unchanged, this problem calls for an experiment. Suppose the librarian were to find at the end of his research project that four week loans result in fifty per cent fewer overdues than two week loans, he would be in a strong position to decide that the length of the loan period is the prime cause of his overdue problem. Here is a schematic of the group comparison design:

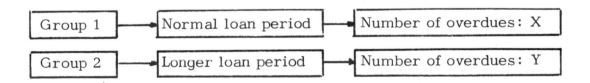

If Y is significantly less than X, if the group with the longer loan period shows fewer overdues, we may assume that lengthening the loan period of books reduces overdues, all else being equal.

This last phrase points up a weakness of the design: What if the two groups were not equal before the comparison? What if Group 1 had happened to be made up of books taken out by slow readers, while Group 2 were books taken out by fast readers? The results could have been the same regardless of loan periods. What this design lacks is control over all independent variables. Experimental research ideally requires that the investigator achieve maximum control over the independent variables.

There is a classic research design that facilitates such control, the randomized four cell design, as it is often called. Here is a schematic:

	Pretest	Experimental variable	Posttest	Difference
Experimental group (E)	A_E	X	B_E	$D_E = B_E - A_E$
Control group (C)	A_C	0	B_C	$D_C = B_C - A_C$

In this design the subjects are assigned at random to groups E and C to obtain equivalence. Before variation, the experimental variable, is introduced in group E a <u>before</u> measure is taken on both groups to confirm that "everything else" is equal. In the diagram this pretest is designated by the letter A. Then the experimental condition is introduced, but only in group E. Finally, an <u>after</u> measure is taken on both groups. The letter B designates this posttest in the diagram. For each group, the difference between posttest and pretest measures (D_E and D_C) are computed. As a last step the difference between the differences ($D_E - D_C$) is found and examined for significance. If found significant, we have very good reason to believe that the experimental condition is the cause of the difference.

An example might look like this. Suppose a new set of filing rules had been developed for the divided catalog. A librarian believes that the new rules are superior to the old rules for the dictionary catalog. If that is correct it follows that library assistants filing by the new rules make fewer errors than assistants using the old rules, given equivalent tasks, conditions, and time limits. But how can this be tested? Perhaps the librarian has at his disposal a group of thirty new students in a training class who are willing to serve as subjects. He might assign fifteen of them at random to the experimental group. The other fifteen are the control group.

Random division of subjects into experimental and control groups serves a very important function: it equalizes unrelated causal factors that may be inherent in members of the total group. In the example, there may be some good filers and some bad filers among the students. Random division will insure that some good and some bad filers will be in both groups. The librarian can now give each of the thirty subjects an equivalent filing task with instructions to file by whatever rules they remember from high school days. He then counts the number of errors, defined as deviations from the library's rules. Both groups are likely to have the same error score since none of the students have had instruction yet.

Now each person is given another equivalent filing task. This time the experimental group is told to use the new rules. The control group must use the old rules. The two groups are carefully kept segregated. At the end of the filing task the errors are counted again. Both groups are likely to have improved materially since even the "bad" old rules are better than no rules at all. But the experimental group can be expected to have improved much more. If the results indeed show a significant difference in the predicted direction the librarian is justified in the conclusion that the difference was caused by the superior quality of the new rules. He can feel quite certain since all other causal factors had been brought under control by randomization. And this control is the hallmark of all good experimental research.

6. STRUCTURE OF DATA

By the time the researcher has formulated his problem, set up his hypotheses, and determined the overall research design he should know what kind of data are needed to carry out the project. If the problem was simply to find out how many books are missing from a collection, and if it had been decided to determine this from a sample, we could visualize the following data structure:

	Criterion: Is this book lost?
First book in sample (accessions number 1)	yes or no
Second book in sample (accessions number 2)	yes or no
⋮	
Last book in sample (accessions number N)	yes or no

A simple count of the yes answers will yield the number of books missing.

If the problem has been to determine the average height of a truck full of books, we could obtain data like these:

	Measurement
Book 1	17 cm
Book 2	23 cm
Book 3	15 cm
and so on	

For each observation there is one measurement. From the total number of measurements an average can be computed, a procedure that will be discussed in chapter 8.

Here is a more complicated data structure. A research report was published some time ago. The project had to do with the differential effects of several warning alternatives on the return rates of overdue books. Three different warning alternatives were tested. The data that were collected looked somewhat like these:

	Criterion: Was this book returned by...		
	...Jan. 1	...Feb. 1	...March 1
Alternative 1			
Borrowed book 1	yes/no	yes/no	yes/no
Borrowed book 2	yes/no	yes/no	yes/no
Borrowed book 3	yes/no	yes/no	yes/no
⋮			
Alternative 2			
Borrowed book 1	yes/no	yes/no	yes/no
⋮			
Alternative 3			
Borrowed book 1	yes/no	yes/no	yes/no
⋮			

Essentially, there was one yes answer for each observation. A comparison of the total number of yes anwers for each alternative yielded the desired information.

Regardless of the research problem and of the design, all conclusions are reached on the basis of data. And all data, ultimately, consist of observations. Observations, in turn, have two components: the thing observed and the property or variable observed. In the last example given the researcher made one observation on book 1 under alternative 1. This was the thing observed. The property observed was the presence or absence on Jan. 1.

In much of research literature the individuals or units on which measurements are taken or on which observations are made are referred to as "subjects" or Ss. We hesitate to use this term in library research because of the special meaning we give to the word "subject". As an alternative we suggest that the set of individuals on which observations are made be called the "system of observed units", or "system" for short.

The second component of an observation, the property by which the observed units vary from each other, is usually called the variable.

Having established that all observations consist of (1) a system of observed units, and (2) of one or more variables, we are in a position to present a general schematic of the structure of data:

System of observed units	Set of observations		
	Variable 1	Variable 2	Variable k
Unit 1	Variate 11	Variate 12	Variate 1k
Unit 2	Variate 21	Variate 22	Variate 2k
⋮	⋮	⋮	⋮
Unit n	Variate n1	Variate n2	Variate nk

This data structure schematic is general. This means that it fits all cases. All library research problems are composed of data that can be resolved, ultimately, to one or several sets of observations that fit this structural pattern. There are no exceptions. Or, said differently, if the data we intend to analyse in a library research project cannot be laid out in this pattern we have not achieved the level of precision requisite for even the simplest fact finding mission. If this happens the problem must be reviewed and the design improved until data are obtained that fit the structural pattern.

Here is an example of a bad data structure. An investigator tried to determine the adequacy of the seating in a given library. He counted the tables and measured the length and width of the room. Let us analyse the data structure. What would the system of observed units be? Perhaps "tables"? If so, what would the variables be? There is nothing to observe! Here is the structure in schematic form:

System	Variable
Table 1	?
Table 2	?
etc.	

Perhaps the observed units are square feet? Look at this data structure:

System	Variable
Square foot 1	?
Square foot 2	?
etc.	

Again, there is nothing to observe, measure, or count. This research project must go back to the drawing board. A look at the data structure tells us that it is not ready for execution.

Having thought about the problem a little more the researcher might add a measure of time (e.g. half hour intervals) and count the number of people seated at each table. The resulting data might look like this:

System	Variable: number of readers (X)		
	Time 1	Time 2	Time k
Table 1	X_{11}	X_{12}	X_{1k}
Table 2	X_{21}	X_{22}	X_{2k}
$\vdots$	$\vdots$	$\vdots$	$\vdots$
Table n	X_{n1}	X_{n2}	X_{nk}

The original problem, adequacy of seating, has now been interpreted in terms of countable table occupancy. This is a significant step toward a concrete answer to the question. And since the data collected fit the general structure developed above the research is assured of being on solid theoretical ground.

The units observed in library science are varied. They may be people for one thing: library patrons, perhaps, or borrowers, or tax payers, or pensioners living in the area served; or librarians, clerks, pages; in any case, persons or individuals on each of whom observations are made. But the units need not always be people. Things can be the basis of research, things such as books, volumes, titles, desks, rooms, libraries, buildings, cities. Often the unit observed is neither a person not a thing but an intangible entity such as a loan transaction, an instance of book use, or an inquiry or question. The nature of the unit does not matter. Any system of units is a legitimate basis for research if it is relevant to the problem at hand and if one or several observations can be made on each unit in the system. In other words, if the system of units

adopted can be measured on at least one variable, and if the resulting
set of observations furthers an inquiry, the investigator is on a solid
methodological basis.

It is important to keep clear the distinction between "system of observed
units" and "variable". Consider this tabulation:

System	Variable
Book 1	12.5 cm
Book 2	17.0 cm
⋮	⋮
Book n	18.0 cm

Here books are the units, centimeters the variables. The measurements
are made on the system "books". Now consider this tabulation:

System	Variable
Library 1	100,000 books
Library 2	200,000 books
⋮	⋮
Library n	150,000 books

Notice that this tabulation also involves books. But now "books" is the
variable. The system is "libraries". In other words, it is possible that
one and the same thing, e.g. books, is the system in one study and the
variable in the next.

Any unit on which an investigator wishes to make an observation, such as
a book, must have some property that can be observed. Often such properties
can be expressed in terms of quantities. If the property is size, for example,
the question "how large is this book?" can be answered by a number: 914
pages, perhaps, or 20 cm tall, or 2 inches thick. Data consisting of
measurements such as these can be tabulated as follows:

Units observed	Size
Book 1	500 pages
Book 2	250 pages
etc	

Size in number of pages is measured on a scale that has an absolute zero point, namely no pages. The scale begins at zero and extends, at least theoretically, to infinity:

0 pages   100 pages   200 pages   300 pages

Quantitative data measured on such a scale are capable of being manipulated mathematically. One can add 500 pages and 250 pages, divide the sum by 2, and arrive at an average of 375 pages. Such data are isomorphic to the arithmetic number system. This scale is often referred to as the "ratio" scale because the ratio between any two numbers is known. In the last example, Book 2 (250 pages long) can be said to be exactly half as large as Book 1 (500 pages long). The ratio of the size of Book 2 to Book 1 is ½.

In contrast, consider the temperatures in two reading rooms. We get two thermometer readings: 50° F and 75° F. But we cannot say that the ratio of the temperature of Room 1 to Room 2 is 2/3. The temperature of the cold room is not two thirds that of the other. These measurements come from a different scale, a scale that lacks the absolute zero point:

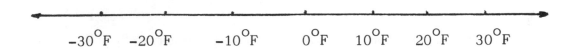

-30°F -20°F -10°F 0°F 10°F 20°F 30°F

Obviously, temperature does not simply stop at 0°F! Zero degrees does not mean absence of temperature as zero pages meant absence of pages. The zero point in the Fahrenheit scale is an arbitrary point. As a consequence 40°F is not twice as warm as 20°F. It is merely 20 degrees warmer. One can also say that the interval between 0° and 20° is the same as that between 20° and 40°. For that reason this scale is often referred to as the "interval" scale of measurement.

The distinction between ratio and interval scales hinges on the fact that the latter measure only intervals, not quantities. Only the difference between two intervals can be computed. Multiplication is not a possible operation with interval measurements. Fortunately for library researchers, division and simpler arithmetic operation can be performed on data measured on either scale. Thus, three books can be measured as follows:

Book 1	11.5 cm tall
Book 2	13.5 cm tall
Book 3	15.0 cm tall
Sum	40.0 cm
Mean	13.3 cm

Likewise, the temperature in three rooms can be measured as follows:

Room 1	64° F
Room 2	60° F
Room 3	71° F
Sum	195°
Mean	65°

The same operations were performed on both sets of data even though they consisted of measurements on different scales.

Some properties are measured in terms of quantities that are infinitely divisible such as time taken to catalog a book. Data like this might be measured in hours, minutes, and seconds. Temperature might be measured to fractions of a degree. These are continuous data. Other data, however, are measured on a coarser scale. A collection has either 12,000 or 12,001 books. There is no finer unit between these two integers. No collection can have 12,000½ books! These are discrete or discontinuous data. Ratio and interval data, wether continuous or discrete, are extremely convenient for research purposes because of their precise mathematical properties.   Unfortunately, they are not very common in the library field. Or rather, while such data are perhaps fairly common, even in the library field, they are usually not very interesting to researchers. We are seldom concerned with the height of books in centimeters. More likely the librarian is concerned with the quality of books or some other non-measurable property.

Methods have been developed, however, to assess non-measurable properties and qualities and express the results in numerical terms. Ranking is one such method. Observed units can be ranked on a scale that distinguishes between more or less of a property. Consider brittleness, for example. It might be possible to compare three specimens of old newspapers and rank them in terms of brittleness. Each specimen would be assigned a value such as least brittle, most brittle, or perhaps medium brittle. Such a brittleness scale might look like this:

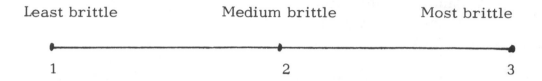

It should be noted that the points on such a scale do not demarcate equal intervals. True, the distance between 1 and 2 appears as large as that between 2 and 3. But this is only because the scale was drawn that way. Here is another brittleness scale:

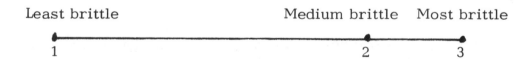

The intervals are now shown to be of different size. But this is of no consequence on a ranking scale. Such a scale accounts only for the order of observations. As long as least, medium, and most brittle are shown in that order the scale is accurate. Data on such a scale are therefore called "ordinal" data.

Even though ordinal measurements are sometimes coded numerically, it must be remembered that such numerical symbols are only codes, not numbers. We might assign the numeral 2 to the class least brittle, and so on. Since these code numbers are arbitrarily assigned any numeral will do as long as the order is preserved. The following two sets of brittleness measurements are equivalent:

	Set 1	Set 2
Newspaper 1	2	2
Newspaper 2	4	5
Newspaper 3	6	10

As long as the order is preserved the magnitude of the code numbers can be changed at will. This is why great care must be exercised in the analysis of opinionaires, rating scales, educational tests, and similar ordinal data. For whenever magnitudes can be changed without affecting the meaning, arithmetic operations performed on such data are mathematically unsound.

There is another important scale to be discussed, the nominal scale. Nominal data merely define identities: a book is not a phonodisc, for example. As far as the distinction between books and phonodiscs is concerned, no other "measurement" can be made. More generally stated, a publication is either a member of the category "books", or it is not. Consider these four objects:

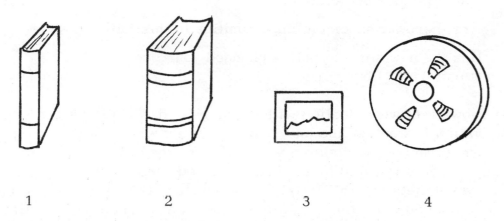

1   2   3   4

Figure 3. Four information storage media

Objects 1 and 2 are members of the category "books". Objects 3 and 4 are not. Since the critical decision point is membership in a category such data are often called categorical data. Categorical data can be tabulated as follows:

Units observed	Member of class "books"?
Object 1	yes or no
Object 2	yes or no
etc.	

Since nominal data are ultimately based on a simple non-numerical binary decision concerning class membership of each unit observed (yes or no) no arithmetic operations can be performed on such data. One can obviously not add 2 yes and 2 no, divide by 4, and obtain a mean of maybe! All one can do, numerically, with data of this quality is to count the total number of successes or yes answers in a given sample of observed units.

Many data in the library field are of this fundamental yes/no pattern. Here are a few examples taken from published research reports:

Is this cross reference from a general to a specific term? yes or no

Has this book been selected by a librarian? yes or no

Is this a theology book? yes or no

Is this library association officer a man? yes or no

Has this book circulated? yes or no

Are there advancement opportunities in this job? yes or no

Has the new service policy changed your
pattern of library use? yes or no

This shows that when dealing with categorical data, all one can say for each observation is whether the unit is or is not a member of the category.

The examples just shown were all in terms of bivariate categories. Many variables fall into more than two categories. Examples are materials for card cabinets (metal, wood, or plastic) and type of employee (teacher, librarian, clerk, or administrator). In general, one can visualize a set of multivariate observations as follows:

	Variable		
System	Category A	Category B	Category C .....
Unit 1	✓		
Unit 2		✓	
⋮			
Unit n			✓

It is important to notice that in such a table the various classes of the variable must be mutually exclusive. Logically, no unit can belong to more than one class or category. There can only be one check mark per unit. The total number of marks must equal n, the number of units observed.

Such data are often summarized by counting the number of check marks recorded for each class and reporting them as frequencies observed. In the example, had n been equal to 40, for example, we might have eleven A's, thirteen B's, and sixteen C's. This summary could be presented in tabular form as follows:

Category	Frequency (f)
A	11
B	13
C	16
	40

It goes without saying that the various classes in such a tabulation must be well defined. Classes or categories such as "newer books", "older books", and "rarities" will not do since the criteria are too vague to be useful. Better: "books published after 1872", "books published between 1501 and 1871", and "books published before 1501".

A common case of poorly defined categories are open ended categories. Consider the following distribution:

Age of books in years	Number of books observed (f)
1 to 5	100
6 to 10	100
11 to 15	50
16 to 20	2
21 to 25	1
26 to 30	1
31 to 35	1
36 to 40	45
	300

This table shows that 45, or almost 1/6 of the books, were 36 years old or older. Now consider the following table, summarizing the same data:

Age of books in years	Number of books observed (f)
0 to 5	100
6 to 10	100
11+	100
	300

This open ended tabulation disguises essential information, namely how old how many of the books are. Such "lying with statistics" usually occurs by accident rather than by design. And while it is not strictly wrong, it is incomplete information and therefore misleading.

To the table with open ended categories we might add the table with lumped categories. Here is an example:

Age of books in years	Number of books observed (f)
0 to 5	100
6 to 10	100
11 to 40	100
	300

Such a table, while not as incomplete as the open ended table, distorts the data in much the same way.

Other complications can arise. A researcher may discover that his data look like this:

1000 Schools in the Survey	
Private control	300
Public control	700
Two year programs	800
Four year programs	200

While the categories in this table are certainly well defined they are not mutually exclusive. The total number of observations adds up to 2000, which is a tell-tale sign that something has gone wrong. There should be no more than 1000 observations. Obviously, this summary table is based on data that consisted of more than one checkmark per unit observed. Or, said differently, the data are based, not on one variable with four classes but on two bivariate variables. Here is a table that reconstructs the data upon which the summary must have been based:

	Variable 1 (Fiscal control)		Variable 2 (Program)	
	Private	Public	Two year	Four year
Unit 1	✓		✓	
Unit 2		✓	✓	
⋮				
Unit n		✓		✓

If this was indeed the structure of the data collected, a better summary table might look like this:

1000 Schools in the Survey		
Private	Two year	200
	Four year	100
Public	Two year	500
	Four year	200

In annual reports of libraries and similar statistical compilations one often encounters examples of misleading statements like this: "The holdings of library X include 50,000 books, a special collection of 2,000 atlases, 300 journal subscriptions, and 1,000 reels of microfilm". If this statement were translated into tabular form the following picture would emerge:

Holdings of X library

Type	Number
Books	50,000
Atlases	2,000
Journals	300
Microfilm (reels)	1,000

Since the 1000 reels of microfilm actually represent 10 journal titles, this table presents an imprecise mixture of different classification principles. A better table might be constructed like this:

Holdings of X library

Books	General	50,000
	Atlases	2,000
Journals	Paper	290
	Microfilm	10

Although the numbers, particularly the count of microfilm holdings, in this last table are a little less impressive, the information is more accurate.

Another requirement for a properly constructed summary table of nominal data is that the categories be exhaustive. The following table shows a flaw in this respect:

70 computer users surveyed

IBM	24
Burroughs	22
Honeywell	11
General Electric	6

Since the total comes to only 63, the four manufacturers in this table, obviously, do not account for all the equipment used by the seventy respondents. Better:

70 computer users surveyed	
IBM	24
Burroughs	22
Honeywell	11
General Electric	6
Other manufacturers	7

Now the tabulation provides a "slot" for each observation, the information is complete.

Whenever observations are made in terms of membership of an observed unit in one or more categories of a variable words such as "yes" or "no" may be used. It is also possible to use check marks. But often numerals are used as symbols, for example "1" in place of "✓" or "yes". As long as the investigator remains consistent and clear to the reader it does not matter which symbols he uses. The following three tables are equivalent:

Table 1. Catalog Style (check marks)

	1. Dictionary	2. Two-way	3. Three-way
Library 1	✓		
Library 2		✓	
Library 3			✓

Table 2. Catalog Style ("yes")

	1. Dictionary	2. Two-way	3. Three-way
Library 1	yes		
Library 2		yes	
Library 3			yes

Table 3. Catalog Style (numeral "1")

	1. Dictionary	2. Two-way	3. Three-way
Library 1	1		
Library 2		1	
Library 3			1

It must be noted that the variate "1" in the last table is used as a label, not as a number or quantity. This distinction is easily overlooked and arithmetic operations are sometimes performed on such labels as if they were numbers. Reports have been published in which data like those in the last table were summarized as follows:

Catalog style	Frequency observed
Dictionary	1
Two-way	2
Three-way	3

What happened was this: the investigator mistook the numerals for numbers and multiplied the label "1" , the variate, with the label for catalog style (1, 2, and 3, respectively), reporting a total of six observations when there were only three. Such faux pas introduce grave distortion into the data and subsequent findings based on them must be regarded with utmost suspicion. For if we have five novels and five plays we have ten pieces of literature. We cannot change this fact even if we use numerals for labels, calling a novel "2" and a play "3". If we say that five novels plus five plays is the same as (5 X 2) + (5 X 3), namely twenty-five pieces of literature, we are clearly wrong. It is therefore of great importance that the library investigator understand the limitations inherent in the kind of data he has at his disposal.

Once the data pertinent to the research project are fully understood and problem and/or hypotheses have been clearly formulated on the basis of solid theoretical guidelines the research design is likely to be sound. Not only that, but the research project is as good as completed! For the hardest part of any research project is the creation of a good design, including a clear plan for the organization of the data. The rest is child's play. Anyone can add and divide numbers. The question is, what do the sums and quotients mean? In the published library literature it is not rare to find such unanswered questions. And more often than not the reason why the question remained unanswered is that the data were collected and evaluated without the benefit of an analysis of the data structure.

7. DATA
    COLLECTION

All research is based on data. All data, in turn, result from observations
of some kind. Observations can be made on several levels. Some events
can be observed at the time they are taking place. Others can only be
studied after they have happened. No event, obviously, can be observed
before it happens. It is possible, then, to visualize all observations as
taking place somewhere on a time line that reaches from the present to the
past:

Present   Yesterday   Past

There is another dimension to be considered. Observations can be made
directly by the researcher in the place where the event is happening. But
some observations cannot be made in this way. Some events must be inferred
from the report of witnesses. The dimension of mediacy can be seen as a
vertical line reaching from direct observation of an event to documentary
evidence of a past event:

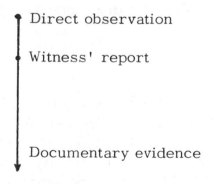

When these two components, the time dimension and the mediacy dimension,
are brought together a true picture of the nature of observations emerges
as follows:

(43)

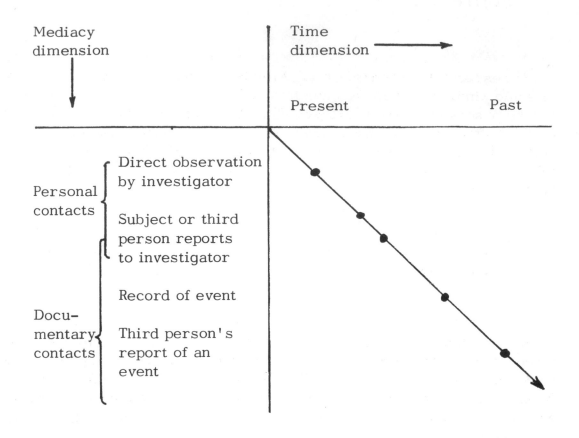

Five points have been marked on the resulting vector because they are the key points in the study of data collection methods. They are taken up one by one on the following pages.

Direct Observation

As any cynic will agree, the job that gets done right is the job you do yourself. So it is with observations. The only fully confidence-inspiring observation is the investigator's own, direct observation of an event at the moment it is happening. There is no possibility of misunderstanding, misstatement, or error due to subjective judgement. From the research design point of view, direct observation is the most desirable data collection method.

Many library phenomena do lend themselves to direct observation. A few years ago a study was published aimed at discovering the seating preferences of library patrons. The researcher collected his data simply by observing a sample of patrons as they seated themselves in the library and took note of where each arrival sat down. After several days of such observations certain preferred seating patterns emerged.

One of the great advantages of direct observation is the possibility of eliminating bias and distortion in the resulting data. A person asked a question, for example, has an opportunity to suppress certain information at will. His response may not be spontaneous. But if the same person is observed (and kept unaware that he is being observed) he cannot possibly modify his behavior in any conscious way. Thus, in the seating preference study mentioned, the investigator obtained a measure of peoples' true seating preferences.

Subject's or Observer's Verbal Report

While some phenomena are easily observed, others are not open to such direct methods. It is one thing to observe where a newly arriving library patron takes his seat. It is quite another problem to observe why he sits there. For such questions researchers often rely on statements made by the observed subject in the course of an interview. Interviewing is a difficult art and whole volumes have been written about its techniques. The main problem with the interview method of data collection is the everpresent danger of introducing unreliability into the data, of contaminating the truth with wishful thinking and deliberate alterations.

There are several levels of contamination. The subject may misunderstand the question. Or the subject may understand the question but misinterpret the connotation of a word or phrase. Careful questioning is required to prevent this from happening.

The subject may understand and interpret the question perfectly but may lack the knowledge required for a good answer. An answer from partial ignorance may sound correct but represents an erroneous opinion.

Or the subject may understand the question, know the answer, and yet mislead the researcher by consciouly avoiding certain truths. To return for a moment to the seating preference question, a patron my have one true reason for seating himself at a certain table: the presence nearby of an attractive member of the opposite sex. In the interview the reason given is likely to be different.

If things in general are not always what they appear to be, the answers or reasons given in an interview, too, are not always the best answers or the real reasons. That is why experienced interviewers go to much trouble planning questions that elicit honest, reliable responses.

Subject's or Observer's Written Report

Often, perhaps too often, even an interview is out of the question. The researcher must rely on peoples' statements sent by mail. This is data collection by questionnaire, a popular method that has, however, more flaws than advantages. There are many reasons for this. As in the interview method, the subject may not understand the question properly. The question may deal with "books". But one respondent may base his answers on "works", a second on sets of books, and a third on volumes. Each of them actually answers a different question but the researcher has no way of knowing this because there is no feedback when the questionnaire method of data collection is employed. The result is a highly unreliable set of data that may or may not mean what they say.

Also, of course, the mail questionnaire respondent may not be equipped to answer the question. This will not be apparent from the return because if there were a way to check on the accuracy of a questionnaire answer the questionnaire would not have been necessary in the first place.

Then there is the problem of misinformation supplied willfully to avoid embarrassment on the part of the respondent. No librarian relishes the prospect of admitting openly that his or her library, for example, is deficient in one or the other area touched upon by the questionnaire. If there is a possible way to interpret a sensitive question in several ways one can assume that each respondent will give the answer that looks best. This is not necessarily a matter of dishonesty. It is only human nature and an expression of the survival instinct.

There is, of course, no sure way of detecting such cases of preverication since the entire data collection process is conducted by mail, without the possibility of cross examining a subject.

Another serious flaw of the questionnaire method of data collection is the problem of returns or yield. Ideally, of one hundred questionnaires mailed, one hundred should be returned for full confidence in the results. Unfortunately, this is seldom if ever achieved. Obviously, the recipient of a questionnaire has the option of not responding. In the simplest case, the non-respondent discards the instrument without reading it. This means that at least he has no special reason not to answer this particular questionnaire. He is simply unwilling to respond, to anything. The second case is more complex. The recipient evaluates the questionnaire and then decides not to answer it. He has a definite reason for ignoring the questionnaire, and this reason often remains unknown to the researcher. The recipient may think the questionnaire is too long, too hard to read, too difficult to answer. In other words, his failure to respond is the fault of the questionnaire. Or he may find that the questions pertain to areas too sensitive, that the answers are too threatening. This is not necessarily a fault of the questionnaire per se. It merely shows that the objective of the research project is very difficult to achieve and that a questionnaire may not be the appropriate method of data collection.

If the questionnaire method is employed to collect data, however, the researcher should always bear in mind that a high rate of return is essential, not just desirable. Consider the case of an investigator who mails 300 questionnaires and receives 160 back. This is more than an academic example since enough cases like that have been reported in the literature. Now suppose one hundred of these returns say "yes" to a certain proposition. Sixty say no. It certainly looks as if the over-whelming majority of the subjects contacted are in favor of that proposition. In truth, however, it is entirely possible, even likely, that the majority of the 140 non-respondents are against the proposition. The actual opinions may actually be distributed like this:

	Recipient's opinion	
	yes	no
Returned	100	60
Not returned	40	100
Totals	140	160

In other words, notwithstanding what the returns seem to say, less than half of the recipients favor the proposition, certainly not the "overwhelming majority" that the limited returns suggest.

Here are five easy points to help questionnaire designers avoid some of the many pitfalls:

1. Ask simple, well-defined questions
2. Avoid superfluous or irrelevant questions
3. Make it short to avoid respondent fatigue
4. Guarantee anonymity to minimize prevarication
5. Mail it to those you know have the answers

Before preparing the big mailing a questionnaire should be tested on a small group to clear up the most obvious misunderstandings. After the mailing a method must be developed for following up on non-respondents. Two or three mail follow-ups are not unusual. If possible, any remaining non-respondents should be contacted by telephone to determine, if nothing else, their bias, their reason for not responding.

Closely related to the questionnaire is the rating form. This is a data gathering instrument that solicits peoples' opinions in a structured way. Each question consists of a "stub" and a scale of graduated or ranked response categories such as this:

	Strongly Agree	Agree	No Opinion	Disagree	Strongly Disagree
The XYZ encyclopedia is one of the most helpful books in the library	☐	☐	☐	☐	☐

The respondent places a checkmark into one of the boxes provided. When all rating forms have been returned the investigator tallies the number of responses received for each of the possible answers.

In general, people tend to favor the answers near the middle of a graduated scale and lean toward the high or favorable end. In the example shown, most answers will probably fall in the second slot from the left, Agree. To overcome the neutralizing effect of such respondent conformity the rating form designer often resorts to the stratagem of the expanded scale. Some favor seven response categories, many think nine are better. Here is a revised version of the encyclopedia question using seven response categories:

	Strong-ly Agree	Agree	Mildly Agree	No Opinion	Mildly Dis-agree	Dis-agree	Strongly Dis-agree
The XYZ encyclopedia is one of the most helpful books in the library	☐	☐	☐	☐	☐	☐	☐

The expanded selection of response categories will now capture the answers of those respondents who truly favor the XYZ encyclopedia under Agree or Strongly Agree, while the answers of those who are merely polite will be concentrated under Mildly Agree or No Opinion. Respondents who truly dislike the XYZ encyclopedia will check Mildly Disagree or Disagree. Few rating form respondents ever check the extremely negative answers. The expanded scale, therefore, yields sharper, more reliable data.

Needless to say, the question or proposition in the stub must be very carefully worded in such a way that all response categories offered apply. Clearly, the following example would be meaningless since the response categories and the question are not compatible:

	Strongly Agree	Agree	Mildly Agree	No Opinion	Mildly Dis-agree	Dis-agree	Strongly Dis-agree
How often do you use the XYZ encyclopedia?	☐	☐	☐	☐	☐	☐	☐

Many variants of the rating form have been devised. One very effective way to force respondent to be definite is the comparison question. Two or more propositions are juxtaposed and the respondent selects one of them as his choice. An example follows.

Which do you consider most suitable for children under 14?	
XYZ encyclopedia	☐
Universal encyclopedia	☐
ABC book of wisdom	☐

Depending on the information desired, such "forced choice" questions can be presented in a variety of combinations and permutations which enables the inventive investigator to build double checks into his rating form by asking the unsuspecting respondent the same question twice, but in different disguises. This yields more reliable information but makes for a larger, more cumbersome rating form.

Record of Event

An event that happened so long ago that no witness remains to be contacted in person or by mail is not necessarily out of the investigator's reach. There are many phenomena in the library world that "speak" through documents. Marion E. Potter and the other editors of the third edition of the United States Catalog of 1912 are probably no longer alive or, if alive, able to answer questions. But the United States Catalog is still here. So while one cannot ask Mrs. Potter what she thought the average historical novel cost in 1912 this information can be culled from the United States Catalog.

Likewise, there are no librarians left who were active in 1910. One cannot get a personal eye witness judgement of the popularity of the works of George Melville Baker in the year 1910. But it is possible to infer such popularity from the publication dates recorded on the catalog cards of a research library, or from other records such as circulation files.

The data obtainable from documents are not restricted to simple facts. By the method of content analysis, for example, even ill-defined characteristics of a document can be expressed quantitatively. To do this the investigator establishes certain categories of concepts relevant to the research. Documents are then read or scanned. A tally is kept of the number of passages the meaning of which coincides with these preestablished categories. In the end the frequencies of instances recorded for each category for a sample of documents yield numerical data that can be used for inferences about phenomena. In a study conducted several years ago Hoffman collected the annual reports of libraries of a certain kind. He established the following categories, among others:

Passage refers to accomplishments in cataloging

Passage refers to accomplishments in circulation work

Passage refers to accomplishments in reference work

As the annual reports were scanned a count was kept of the number of lines devoted to each of these categories. The result showed that an extraordinarily large proportion of space was devoted to accomplishments in cataloging and circulation work, activities that lend themselves to easy measurement. Almost no space was given to the accomplishments in reference work. This state of affairs, incontrovertibly established by documentary evidence, served as a basis for inferences about the value of annual reports as library evaluation tools.

Report of a Long Past Event

The evaluation of a third person's report of something that happened long ago yields data that are, in terms of mediacy, at the opposite end from direct observation. Typically, such secondary data are collected from books, magazines, and similar publications. A historical researcher trying to recreate or interpret the spirit of 1876 would rely heavily on journalistic reports of what Dewey and others said in their speeches. Obviously, hearing a speech is one thing. Telling what the speaker said, or relating what those who heard him say he said, is another thing. Such data are rich sources, not only for objective information but also for subjective judgement, bias, artful addition, or purposeful omission. The use of secondary data, therefore, requires considerable interpretive skill and background knowledge. An inexperienced person will find it difficult to distinguish fact from fancy in what he is reading.

What data collection method is best? That is hard to say. Much depends on the nature of the phenomenon studied. In general, the vector of page 44 is a good guideline: the closer the data collection method comes to the origin of the vector line, the better suited the method is for the study under consideration.

DESCRIPTIVE STATISTICS

8 DATA DISPLAY
AND
SUMMARY STATISTICS

Suppose an investigator collected data concerning the number of times each of 41 books circulated before the binding broke. The data from this hypothetical project are given in the following table:

Number of times circulated before binding broke

24	34	25	66	77	35	26	58	54	46	52
73	67	78	61	65	38	70	54	57	49	29
46	68	28	45	47	60	42	50	62	56	61
63	72	69	71	74	55	69	50			

A table of data like these makes tedious reading if reported without any further attempt at organization. The table becomes many times more useful if the data are arranged in rank order from lowest to highest:

Number of times circulated before binding broke

24	25	26	28	29	34	35	38	42	45	46
46	47	49	50	50	52	54	54	55	56	57
58	60	61	61	62	63	65	66	67	68	69
69	70	71	72	73	74	77	78			

Rank ordering of the same data enables the reader to see that the data ranged from 24 at the lowest to 78 at the highest point, and that the middle value was 56 circulations.

The same table can be condensed to provide an even more compact summary of the data. Instead of reporting 41 cases the investigator lumps the scores into a few groups and then counts and reports the number of cases

(54)

that fall into each group. The result is what is known as a frequency distribution. In the construction of a frequency distribution the first question is how many groups one should have, and what range of values one should have in each group, or class interval, as the technical term goes. A rule of thumb is that one should have about ten intervals with from 3 to 10 score points each. In our case, we have data ranging from 24 to 78; this is a span of 54 score points. We can conveniently group these into eleven intervals of 5 scores each:

Class intervals	f
24 – 28	4
29 – 33	1
34 – 38	3
39 – 43	1
44 – 48	4
49 – 53	4
54 – 58	6
59 – 63	5
64 – 68	4
69 – 73	6
74 – 78	3
	41

In constructing a frequency distribution care must be taken to avoid overlapping groups. The following set of intervals, for example, would cause a problem when a score of 30 is observed:

1. 20 – 25
2. 25 – 30
3. 30 – 35
4. 35 – 40

Where should one record 30 – in interval 2 or in interval 3? An impossible decision! Better to regroup the data:

1. 20 – 24
2. 25 – 29
3. 30 – 34
4. 35 – 39

Now there is a definite place for every observation. The value 30 belongs into the third group, nowhere else.

Frequency distributions are much used for the organization of research data in all fields. One of the reasons for their popularity is the ease with which they can be converted to graphs. Graphs or plots are most helpful in visualizing a situation described by quantitative data. Here is a graph representing the circulation per binding data given in the table at the top of page 55:

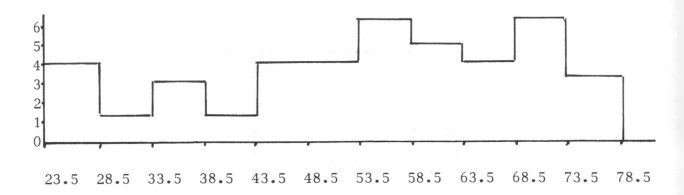

23.5   28.5   33.5   38.5   43.5   48.5   53.5   58.5   63.5   68.5   73.5   78.5

Figure 4. Histogram

This graph, composed of rectangles whose width represents the class intervals and whose height stands for the frequencies goes under the name of "histogram", a coinage from history and the Greek word for writing. It is a visualization or record of the history of a set of data, as it were. Notice that the points on the abscissa or X axis are the "true" boundaries between intervals. The boundary between the first and the second class interval, for example, is considered to be 28.5, the halfway point between 28 and 29. The boundary between the second and the third intervals is 33.5, and so on.

Histograms appear frequently in research reports but not as often as frequency polygons, a similar graphic method of summarizing and visualizing tables of data. The frequency polygon is based on the midpoints of the class intervals. The midpoint of the interval 24 – 28, for example, is 26. Here are the same fictitious data again with class midpoints: :

Class intervals	Midpoints	f
24 – 28	26	4
29 – 33	31	1
34 – 38	36	3
39 – 43	41	1
44 – 48	46	4
49 – 53	51	4
54 – 58	56	6
59 – 63	61	5
64 – 68	66	4
69 – 73	71	6
74 – 78	76	3
		41

To construct the graph the midpoints are plotted on the abscissa and the
frequencies on the ordinate. The resulting points in the coordinate system
are then connected by straight lines to yield the curve. At either end of the
curve is a zero frequency point as shown in figure 5.

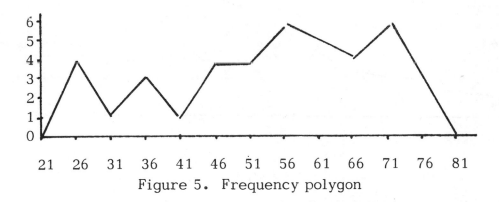

21   26   31   36   41   46   51   56   61   66   71   76   81

Figure 5. Frequency polygon

The frequency polygon is found in many research reports, but still more
often one encounters a further refinement: the cumulative frequency polygon.
This graph is also based on the midpoints of the class intervals. But instead
of the simple frequency, the corresponding cumulated group frequency is
plotted over the midpoint value on the abscissa. To cumulate the observed
frequencies in a distribution one simply adds all the frequencies in
succession. When the resulting points from this operation are plotted and
connected by straight lines the characteristic ogive results. Here, once
more, are the same data, this time as a cumulative frequency distribution:

Class intervals	Midpoints	cf
24 – 28	26	4
29 – 33	31	5
34 – 38	36	8
39 – 43	41	9
44 – 48	46	13
49 – 53	51	17
54 – 58	56	23
59 – 63	61	28
64 – 68	66	32
69 – 73	71	38
74 – 78	76	41

The corresponding graph is constructed by plotting the midpoints against the cumulated frequencies:

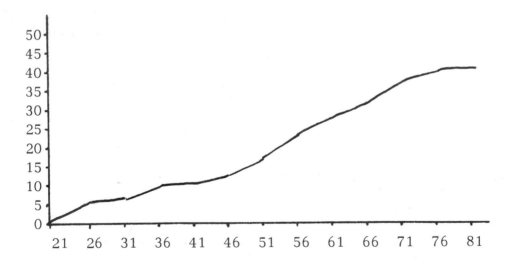

Figure 6. Cumulative frequency polygon

This cumulative frequency polygon or ogive is often used to advantage for comparison purposes. Suppose Library X was one of four comparable institutions in a region and there was reason to point out that the pattern of book usage in Library X differed significantly from the patterns of the other three libraries. An investigator has drawn a random sample of books from each library's collection and noted for each book in the samples the number of years elapsed since last circulation. Here are the fictitious data:

Years since last circulated	Midpoint	Library A		Library B		Library C		Library X	
		f	cf	f	cf	f	cf	f	cf
0 – 4	2	2	2	3	3	2	2	30	30
5 – 9	7	6	8	5	8	4	6	22	52
10 –14	12	5	13	6	14	7	13	18	70
15 –19	17	8	21	9	23	10	23	10	80
20 –24	22	12	33	11	34	11	34	10	90
25 –29	27	20	53	19	53	18	52	10	100
30 –34	32	50	103	40	93	45	97	5	105

Nothing shows the essential difference between Library X and the other three institutions quite as drastically as the comparative cumulative frequency polygons of figure 7:

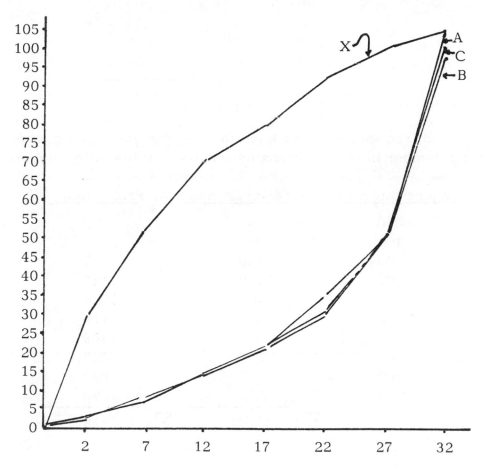

Figure 7. Four frequency polygons superimposed for comparison.

60

It is often helpful for comparison purposes to convert frequencies into proportions or percentages. An investigator might wish to know, for example, how many books in a sample fall into each of ten subject categories. The following table shows a set of fictitious data of this kind:

Subject Category	Number of books in a sample that fell into each of ten subject categories
000	60
100	200
200	150
300	400
400	160
500	300
600	200
700	350
800	650
900	250
	2720

Such observed frequencies are easier to compare when shown as proportions of the total number of observations as was done in the following table:

Subject category	Observations	Proportions
000	60	.022
100	200	.073
200	150	.055
300	400	.147
400	160	.058
500	300	.110
600	200	.073
700	350	.129
800	650	.239
900	250	.092
Σ f : 2720		Σ p : .998

The proportion p of a given class interval in a frequency distribution can be seen as the quotient of the observed class frequency f divided by the total of all observed frequencies, Σf. This proportion is easily converted into the slightly more convenient percentage P by multiplying the same quotient by 100:

$$P = 100 \ (f/\Sigma f)$$

Here are the same data as percentages:

Subject category	Observations	Percentages
000	60	2.2
100	200	7.35
200	150	5.51
300	400	14.7
400	160	5.88
500	300	11.02
600	200	7.35
700	350	12.86
800	650	23.89
900	250	9.19
	2720	99.95

Display in the form of percentages makes it much easier to compare two or more sets of data. Consider the following data:

Expenditure data for two kinds of libraries (fictitious)

	Type A Percentage of total expenditures	Type B Percentage of total expenditures
Salaries	65.6	49.2
Materials	17.0	33.4
Binding	1.2	3.8
Other	16.2	13.6
	100.0	100.0

An effective way to visualize such comparative percentages is the pie shaped graph. In a pie graph the total circle of 360 degrees represents 100 per cent. To find the number of degrees corresponding to a given percentage one simply multiplies the percentage value by a factor of 3.6. Thus, 17 per cent corresponds to 61.2 degrees (17 X 3.6 = 61.2) in the circular graph. Figure 8 shows two such graphs for the expenditure data given in the preceding table:

Figure 8. Pie graphs showing relative percentages

It goes without saying that care must be taken with the decimal point when converting frequencies to proportions and to percentages. One must especially guard against the mistake of intermingling proportions with percentages in the same table or graph. Nothing can lead to misunderstandings easier than a table of data headed "Percentages" in which the data are actually proportions while the corresponding text speaks of frequencies. When in such a table the value "0.1" appears without explanation a reader is at a loss: does this mean ten per cent or is it the equivalent of the proportion "0.001"?

Measures of central tendency

The main thrust of all true research is to observe, describe, and make statements about a group or aggregate of animate or inanimate subjects. Seldom if ever is a researcher interested in the specific fate of one single individual. In statistical terminology such aggregates are referred to as populations. When we study a population we take one observation on each member of the population. The resulting data can be displayed in the form of an array or table:

Ranked list of 43 fictitious scores

```
24  45  48  53  55  60  78
25  46  48  54  56  61
28  46  48  54  56  62
29  47  50  54  57  65
39  47  51  54  58  66
42  48  51  55  58  76
43  48  52  55  59  76
```

It is cumbersome, to say the least, to read a large array of data like these, and it is very difficult to make concise statements about them. For that reason the researcher usually tries to describe the obtained measurements by way of a summary statistic, a measure of central tendency. There are several such measures in common use. The three that are most often found in research reports are the mode, the median, and the mean.

The first of these three averages, the mode, is a score value. For an array of data such as those given above the mode answers the question: which is the most frequently occurring score? It is found simply by inspection. In the example, no other score value appears as often as 48. Hence 48, the value that occurs five times, is the mode of that distribution.

Not all distributions are limited to a single mode. Here is a hypothetical bimodal distribution:

Score	Frequency
35	3
34	8
33	2
32	1
31	8
30	3

The two modes are 31 and 34. Both values occur eight times.

More important than the mode is the second average, the median . The median is the middle value in an ordered series of scores. For the 43 rank ordered scores shown above the median, 53, is found simply by counting to 22 from either end. In a rank ordered list of 43 scores the

22nd value is the middle value, also called the 50th percentile. If we let N stand for the number of observations, and N is odd, we can define the median as the $((N+1)/2)$th score. If N is even, we can define the median as the value that lies half way between the $(N/2)$th and the $(N/2 + 1)$th score.

When the median is known one can say certain things about the distribution. For example, half the observations shown in the table at the top of page 63 have a score value of 53 or higher. As a summary statistic, the median is somewhat limited, however. The median says nothing, for example, about the upper limit of the scores above the median. The distribution at the top of page 63 reaches its highest point at 78. Had this value been 780 instead, the median would still be 53! This statistic, we say, is insensitive to extreme score values.

This is one reason why researchers usually prefer the third of the averages, the arithmetic mean. The mean, sometimes carelessly referred to as "the average", is perhaps the single most important of all statistics. It is very simple in concept. It is also basic to so many statistical methods of data analysis that no progress in quantitative research is thinkable without it. The mean, as we have indicated, is simple to compute. First, one adds up the values of the measurements (X). Schematically, this operation can be shown as follows:

$$
\begin{array}{ll}
\hline
& \text{Variable (X)} \\
\hline
\text{Observation 1:} & X_1 \\
\text{Observation 2:} & X_2 \\
\quad\quad \vdots \\
\text{Observation n:} & X_n \\
\hline
& \sum_{i=1}^{n} X_i
\end{array}
$$

Next, one divides the sum by the number of observations (N):

$$
\text{Mean, } \bar{X} \text{ (ex bar)} = \frac{\sum_{i=1}^{n} X_i}{N}
$$

This equation or formula is often presented in simplified form:

$$\overline{X} = \frac{\sum X}{N}$$

For the data at the top of page 63 the mean can now be computed as follows:

$$\overline{X} = \frac{\sum X}{N} = \frac{2227}{43} = 51.79$$

As most other things in life, the mean has a few drawbacks. The most important of these is perhaps the fact that the arithmetic mean, as its name suggests, requires the performance of arithmetic operations (addition and division) on the variates from which it is computed. And arithmetic operations can be performed properly only on numbers of interval quality or better. Thus the mean can be computed for ratio data such as these:

Units observed	Variable (Age in years)
Book 1	7 years
Book 2	8 years
Book 3	5 years
Book 4	4 years
	24 years

$$\text{Mean, } \overline{X} = \frac{24}{4} = 6 \text{ years}$$

But the mean cannot be computed for categorical data such as those shown on the next page:

Units observed	Variable (Does book have plastic cover?)	
	Verbal	Coded
Book 1	yes	1
Book 2	no	2
Book 3	no	2
Book 4	yes	1

Notice that the numbers in the right hand column are only code symbols. They have no numerical value. One cannot meaningfully add them to obtain a sum of 6 which, when divided by 4, yields a mean of 1.5. A mean of 1.5 "what", one would have to ask. Obviously, such numbers make no sense.

When the mean must be computed for large numbers of observations, elaborate formulas have been developed for its computation from grouped data. With the advent of large and small electronic computers these older manual methods have become obsolete. We shall say more about the computer in Appendix 1.

Measures of dispersion

On page 63 we presented a set of 43 scores which we described in summary form by a statistic, the median of 53. But due to its insensitivity to extreme values we found that the median does not always tell the full story. Consider the two sets of data shown in the following table:

Group I	Group II
1	1
3	4
7	7
13	90
20	116

The two sets of data are not equally dispersed around the median, 7 in both cases. To describe these two groups of data more fully we need another summary statistic, one that describes the dispersion of the data.

A suitable measure of dispersion for these data is the range. The range can be defined as the difference between the highest and the lowest score in a distribution. The data in Group I above range from 1 to 20. The data in Group II range from 1 to 116. We might report the following summary statistics:

Group I:	Group II:
Median = 7	Median = 7
Range = 19	Range = 115

Complete summary statistics like these alert the reader to the fact that the two distributions described did differ in spite of equal medians.

The mean does not always tell the whole truth either. Let us assume a researcher wants to test the hypothesis that the average woman librarian receives less pay than the average man. The researcher might collect the following data   (salaries in thousands of dollars):

	Female librarians	Male librarians
	10.0	14.0
	10.6	14.0
	12.0	15.6
	12.0	16.0
	33.0	18.0
	34.0	34.0
Σx :	111.6	111.6
$\overline{X}$:	18.6	18.6

The researcher could justify the conclusion that as far as his samples show, the two classes of librarians earn equivalent salaries as measured by the arithmetic mean. But can he conclude, therefore, that women had equal chances, salary-wise, as men? Of course not. The distributions differ so much in their dispersion around the mean that one can see by simple inspection of the data that a woman's chances of getting paid $14,000 or more are much smaller than those of a man's. In fact, more than half of all the women in the sample earn less money than even the lowest paid man! Notice that the mean did not divulge all this information. We need another statistic to summarize the dispersion.

The most useful measure of variability for data of this quality is the standard deviation. This statistic is based on individual score deviations from the mean of their distribution. Schematically, we can show a distribution as follows:

Schematic of a Distribution

	Scores, X	Score deviations from the mean, $X-\overline{X}$ or x	Squared deviations, x^2
SS_1	X_1	x_1	x_1^2
SS_2	X_2	x_2	x_2^2
.	.	.	.
.	.	.	.
.	.	.	.
SS_n	X_n	x_n	x_n^2
	$\sum_{i=1}^{n} X_i$		$\sum_{i=1}^{n} x_i^2$

This distribution has a mean:

$$\overline{X} = \frac{\sum_{i=1}^{n} X_i}{N}$$

A little reasoning will make it clear that each observed score deviates from this mean by a certain amount. This is shown schematically in the column headed $X-\overline{X}$ or x. Since we are interested in a measure that would describe the distribution in terms of an average deviation of the scores from the mean nothing seems simpler than to repeat the process we employed with the raw scores when we computed the mean: add them all up and divide the sum by N. However, we find that by the nature of the mean as a balancing point, some of our deviation scores are positive, some are negative. In fact, when we add them up,

$$\sum_{i=1}^{n} x_i$$

we find that the result is always zero. And we can, of course, not work with a sum of zero.

But statisticians have devised a stratagem. They simply square the deviation scores. This operation, shown in column x^2 of the schematic, eliminates all negative numbers among the x values. The sum of the squared deviation scores, therefore, is always greater than zero.

In order to obtain an average of the deviations from the mean this sum is now divided by the degrees of freedom of the deviation scores, N-1:

$$\frac{\sum_{i=1}^{n} x_i^2}{N-1}$$

The resulting quotient goes by the name of "the variance". The divisor is called the "degrees of freedom" for the following reason. The sum of the deviation scores (Σx) in any distribution is zero. This means that when 9 out of ten deviation scores are known the 10th is no longer free to vary, it is known. Where N equals 10, therefore, 9 scores, or N-1, are free to vary. In such a distribution there are 9 degrees of freedom, as the technical term goes.

One last hurdle is left to conquer. Since the variance is an average in terms of squares, but we want to say things about the distribution in terms of the original measurements, we must take the square root of that expression. The square root of the variance, however, is the standard deviation

$$s = \sqrt{\frac{\sum_{i=1}^{n} x_i^2}{N-1}}$$

For the salary data of page 67 we can now show the standard deviations. First the women:

Salary data for female librarians (fictitious)

	X	x	x^2
SS_1	10	−8.6	73.96
SS_2	10.6	−8	64.00
SS_3	12	−6.6	43.56
SS_4	12	−6.6	43.56
SS_5	33	14.4	207.36
SS_6	34	15.4	237.16
			669.6

$\overline{X} = 18.6$

$$s^2 \text{ (variance)} = \frac{669.6}{5} = 133.92$$

$$s = \sqrt{133.92} = 11.57$$

The standard deviation for the men is, of course, computed in the same way. The value comes to s = 7.68. We are now in a position to report the fictitious salary research results in summary form:

Female librarians
Mean: $18,600.00
Standard
deviation: 11,570.00

Male librarians
Mean: $18,600.00
Standard
deviation: 7,680.00

It is customary procedure to report the standard deviation along with the mean in all descriptive quantitative research.

In real life distributions are bound to be much more voluminous than the simple examples we have shown. The associated calculations would soon become prohibitively laborious if attempted in the way we have done here. The reader is referred to Appendix 1 for a discussion of computer methods as labor saving devices.

9. CORRELATION

Summary statistics describing one set of observations in terms of a certain variable are very useful in library research as elsewhere, as we have shown in the previous chapter. We must now concern ourselves with a slightly different research situation. It involves the calculation of summary statistics describing the relationship between more than one set of observations. Consider the theory that, as libraries grow larger, users lose touch with the staff. In other words, while a library rich in books will obviously be able to serve its users better than a poor library, it may also be true that increased size of a library's collection is detrimental to user activity. And that may be of importance in the light of the considerations on which a certain research project is based.

To test the presumed relationship between collection size and user activity a researcher might obtain two measures from each of one hundred libraries. The first measure is collection size, obtained by counting the volumes held. The second measure is user activity expressed in terms of the average number of questions asked per opening hour. The purely fictitious data are presented in the following table:

X	Y	X	Y	X	Y	X	Y	X	Y
23468	7	76497	15	85147	19	77764	12	79847	12
32845	14	73497	10	67456	3	66612	3	54759	19
80499	19	99141	15	32676	9	33731	7	69014	17
78350	15	48533	2	73390	7	42193	3	60939	3
45368	15	93363	19	37892	11	60316	9	99342	9
42068	6	21846	12	76590	12	29166	1	95304	16
43117	5	41320	15	28342	10	40582	4	93983	11
36547	14	45713	4	38816	14	42947	10	75733	4
21347	5	31525	9	64658	4	56085	13	23856	9
44860	5	68821	13	46682	10	69137	16	63005	19
41787	17	66099	2	47332	2	38993	8	92279	14
36095	2	53925	10	68244	16	93321	19	45045	4
62800	9	97830	10	52322	12	37537	6	23384	14
30175	4	33379	4	94734	14	25653	7	20788	13
93913	13	37280	3	67948	7	29384	7	72715	10
46721	12	89916	8	99282	11	99760	16	20342	2
89190	15	36403	9	55400	19	23774	13	48145	9
43322	6	59716	15	32620	7	40685	3	30929	6
49812	12	38247	2	90983	13	63071	13	39996	14
77642	15	53284	13	93211	13	60335	18	73942	7

These data are technically an accurate description of the relationship between X and Y. But in this form the overall picture is hard, if not impossible, to see. The same information might be more advantageously displayed graphically as in the scatter plot that follows.

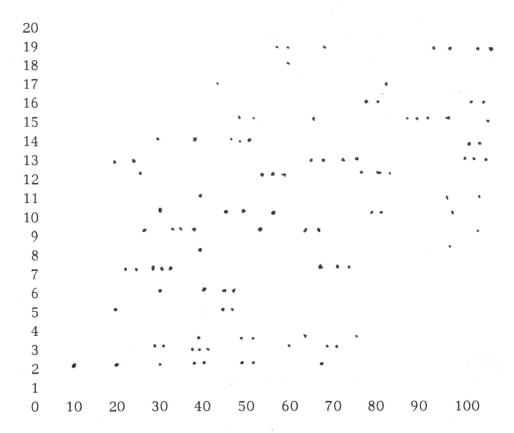

However, even here we can see that one hundred points in a system of coordinates do not necessarily create a much clearer picture. What we need is another summary statistic that would express the nature of the relationship between collection size and user activity.

Before we go much further along this line of reasoning we should take time to reflect that this relationship has two components. The first of these is quickly explained. If there is any noticeable relationship at all between collection size and user activity in the libraries studied then this relationship must either be positive or negative. This means that user activity increases with increasing collection size, or it decreases. The relationship may take either direction. Graphically, these two situations can be shown as in the next figure. The graph on the left shows positive correlation, the graph on the right negative.

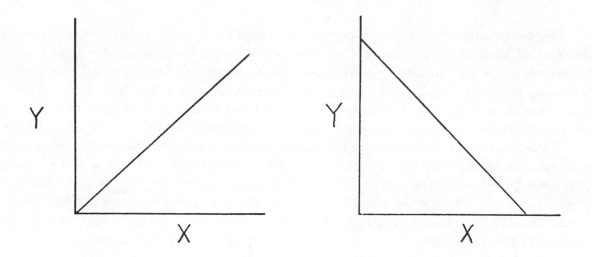

However, we are not so much concerned with the direction than with the strength of the relationship under discussion. Let us retreat to a smaller, artificially contrived example for pedagogical reasons. Consider the following data:

	X	Y
Subject 1	1	2
Subject 2	3	4
Subject 3	5	6
Subject 4	7	8

The reader will notice that these data have been selected so as to be obvious: a case of perfect correlation. Now let us demonstrate what we mean by "perfect". The only thing that makes this example, or any case in the real world, worth studying is the fact that the observations vary from each other. And we saw earlier that such variation can be described mathematically in terms of deviations from the mean, or more practically, in terms of the squares of such deviations. The by now familiar transformation of observations to deviation scores has been performed and the resulting data are given in the following table:

	X	x	x^2	Y	y	y^2
Ss1	1	−3	9	2	−3	9
Ss2	3	−1	1	4	−1	1
Ss3	5	1	1	6	1	1
Ss4	7	3	9	8	3	9

Mean, $\overline{X} = 4$; $\overline{Y} = 5$
Sum of squared deviation scores, $\sum x^2 = 20$; $\sum y^2 = 20$

The two sums of squares together represent the total theoretically possible amount of variation for the distribution. But since the sums of squares were taken variable by variable -- first all the X values alone, then all the Y values -- they say nothing about the relationship between X and Y for any of the four individuals or subjects studied. To obtain a measure of that part of the variation we must study the variation when taken on an observation by observation basis.

Mathematically this is done by obtaining the cross products of the deviation scores. In other words, for each subject or observed unit the x and y values are multiplied with each other. The sum of these cross products can be inter- preted as a measure of the total observed variation, as opposed to the total theoretically possible variation. The entire operation lends itself to a graphical demonstration. In column 5 of the following table we have computed the cross products for the same data:

	1	2	3	4	5
	X	x	Y	y	xy
Ss1	1	−3	2	−3	9
Ss2	3	−1	4	−1	1
Ss3	5	1	6	1	1
Ss4	7	3	8	3	9
					20

The sum of the cross products is 20. We would like to express this observed total variation as a proportion of the theoretically possible variation.

The reasoning behind this is straightforward. If the relationship between X and Y were perfect, then we would know that for every change in X there is an equivalent change in Y. This means that knowledge of the variation in X enables us to predict with complete certainty the variation in Y. Or, said differently, all the variation in Y can be explained by variation in X. In our simplified example we already know by inspection that we have a perfect, positive relation- ship between X and Y. It remains for us to complete the graphic demonstration of how variation in Y can be explained by variation in X.

Let us show the sum of the cross products (20) and the sums of the squares (20 each) as lines, as in figure 9:

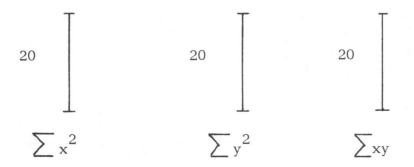

Figure 9. Sums of squares and cross products

These lines say nothing, so far, about the relationship between X and Y. But we can get a picture of the relationship if we convert the lines into squares as in figure 10.

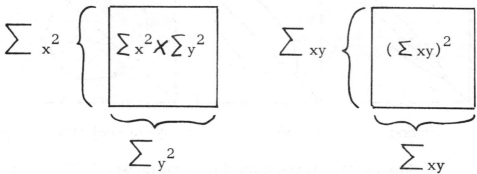

Figure 10. Theoretical and observed variation

The square on the left represents the total theoretically possible variation, in this case 20 X 20 = 400. The square on the right represents the total observed variation, in this case also 20 X 20 = 400. Now then, since we want to express the observed variation as a proportion of the theoretically possible variation, all we have to do is to divide the right hand square, $(\Sigma xy)^2$, by the left hand square, $\Sigma x^2 \times \Sigma y^2$. Or in numbers, 400/400, which equals 1. This quotient says directly what proportion of the total variation the observed variation is, namely all of it, 1.00!

Actually, this is no surprise since we set up the data this way on purpose. This quotient, by the way, goes under the name of coefficient of determination. Its symbol is r^2. This coefficient can be shown as a formula:

$$r^2 = \frac{(\Sigma xy)^2}{\Sigma x^2 \times \Sigma y^2}$$

The r^2 coefficient indicates how much of the variation in Y is explained by variation in X.

In real life, of course, correlation is seldom if ever perfect. More often than not, the points of a scatter plot distribute themselves in the shape of an ellipse rather than a straight line. We can interpret the width of that ellipse as an indicator of the strength of the relationship: the narrower the ellipse, the higher the correlation; and the fatter the ellipse, the lower the correlation. Figure 11 shows graphically three patterns of correlation of different strength:

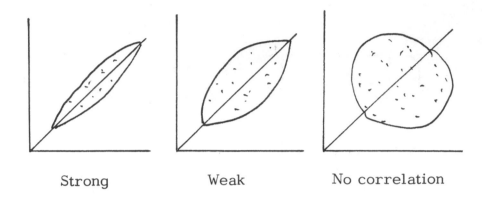

| Strong | Weak | No correlation |

Figure 11. Three correlation patterns.

We will now present an example that will result in a coefficient of determination that is less than 1.

| | (1) | (2) | (3) | (4) | (5) | (6) | (7) |
	X	x	x^2	Y	y	y^2	xy
Ss1	1	−3	9	2	−3	9	9
Ss2	3	−1	1	4	−1	1	1
Ss3	5	1	1	8	3	9	3
Ss4	7	3	9	6	1	1	3
Sums	16	0	20	20	0	20	16

If we insert the sums from this table into our formula for the coefficient of determination we obtain

$$r^2 = \frac{(\sum xy)^2}{\sum x^2 \times \sum y^2} = \frac{16^2}{20 \times 20} = \frac{256}{400} = .64$$

In other words, the correlation in this example is less than 1, less than perfect. In fact, only 64% of the variation in Y is accounted for by variation in X. Or, 36% of the variation remains unexplained.

Partly for mathematical reasons and partly by tradition the relationship between two such variables is usually reported in the literature in terms of the square root of the coefficient of determination, the socalled Pearson's r. We can derive the formula for Pearson's r quite easily from what we already know:

$$r = \frac{\sum xy}{\sqrt{\sum x^2 \times \sum y^2}}$$

where x and y, as before, are deviation scores.   This correlation coefficient r which, by the way, requires data that can be added, multiplied, and divided, extends from a maximum of +1 or –1 (positive or negative perfect correlation) to no correlation at all, represented by a coefficient of r = 0. The r coefficient, then, is the summary statistic that expresses the nature (positive or negative) and the strength of the relationship between two variables. For the large table of data given on page 71 the r coefficient comes to 0.41. This number says what the scatter plot of page 72 tried to say. And this graphic will help the reader understand that a correlation coefficient of r = .41 represents and association that is not very strong. Anyone who studies the scatter plot of page 72 can see that a measurement taken at point 60 on the abscissa or x axis may correspond to 3, or 13, or 19 on the ordinate or y axis. In other words, knowledge of X tells the investigator very little about Y. It could be low, or high, or middling. As a guideline we suggest the following ranges for the interpretation of a correlation coefficient:

r	unexplained variation	interpretation
0 to .5	75% or more	weak correlation
.5 to .7	50% to 75%	moderate correlation
.7 to .8	33% to 50%	substantial correlation
.8 to1.0	33% or less	strong correlation

Why does the correlation coefficient reach its maximum value at $r = 1$? Why cant't there be a coefficient greater than unity? The reason is conveniently demonstrated by means of another, closely related statistic, Spearman's rank correlation coefficient, ρ (Greek rho, also called r_S).

This coefficient, as its name indicates, utilizes data of ordinal quality that do not lend themselves to the operations of addition and division but can be rank ordered. Here is a set of such rank ordered data:

	(1)	(2)	(3)	(4)	(5)	(6)
	X	Rank X	Y	Rank Y	d	d^2
Ss1	2	1	10	1	0	0
Ss2	4	2	15	2	0	0
Ss3	6	3	20	3	0	0
Ss4	8	4	25	4	0	0
Ss5	10	5	30	5	0	0

Here the quantity d stands for the difference between ranks, Rank X – RankY. The fictitious data show that for each Subject the difference between column 2 and column 4 is zero. Consequently, the square of d is also zero, and the sum of the squared differences, naturally, is zero, too. This is so because the data have been made up in such a way that the highest rank on X is paired with the highest rank on Y, and the lowest rank on X with the lowest rank on Y. We can expect the highest, most perfect positive correlation coefficient possible. Here, then, are the calculations. The rho coefficient is defined by this formula:

$$r_S = 1 - \frac{6 \sum d^2}{N^3 - N}$$

Substituting the data from the table we have:

$$r_S = 1 - \frac{6 \times 0}{125 - 5} = 1 - 0 = 1$$

This is what $r_S = 1$ means. There is no higher value possible since correlation cannot be more perfect than perfect.

The coefficient in the previous example was positive because high rank was paired with high rank, and low rank with low rank. Now for an example in which we should expect maximum negative correlation.

	(1)	(2)	(3)	(4)	(5)	(6)
	X	Rank X	Y	Rank Y	d	d^2
Ss1	2	1	30	5	–4	16
Ss2	4	2	25	4	–2	4
Ss3	6	3	20	3	0	0
Ss4	8	4	15	2	2	4
Ss5	10	5	10	1	4	16

Obviously, high rank is now paired with low, and low with high. We can expect a negative coefficient. Also, the correlation is perfect. We should predict a rho coefficient of –1. Here are the calculations.

$$r_S = 1 - \frac{6 \sum d^2}{N^3 - N} = 1 - \frac{6 \times 40}{125 - 5} = 1 - \frac{240}{120} = 1 - 2 = -1$$

The rho coefficient is indeed as predicted, –1. This simple demonstration should have convinced the reader that correlation coefficients go from –1 to +1 at the most. No lower or higher values are possible.

The discussion so far should also have made it clear that for a proper correlation study it is necessary to investigate the relationship between at least two variables. In fact, correlation between two variables, or "bivariate" correlation, is what most people think of when they speak of correlation. For the record, it must be pointed out here that in addition to the well-known bivariate correlation methods -- Pearson's r, Spearman's rho, and many others -- there are also a variety of multivariate correlation procedures, procedures that account for the simultaneous association between three or more variables. The need for these methods arises whenever a variable under study can be presumed to be related not only to one but to many other variables. One such multivariate statistic is the multiple correlation coefficient $R_{Z.XY}$. This coefficient, which also extends from –1 to +1, defines the degree of association between the combination of two independent variables X and Y with a dependent variable Z.

The variables in any correlation study must fulfill certain requirements. Not only must they be measurements or counts on a scale appropriate for the particular coefficient under consideration -- ratio quality data for

Pearson's r, ordinal quality data for Spearman's rho -- but they must also be observations made on subjects that represent a homogeneous population. The subjects under study should be as much alike as possible in all respects except for the variables under consideration. To give a crass example, correlation of height and weight computed from measurements taken on a book, an audio cassette, a filmstrip, and a phonodisc is meaningless if only because the subjects on which the observations were made, while all information storage media, are not a homogeneous population. Better: the same computation based on measurements taken on four books. While this might still not yield overly useful information it has at least the virtue of being methodologically sound.

Another requirement for a correlation study is that all observations be made on each of the subjects under study. Schematically, we can represent such a set of data as follows:

	X	Y
Observed unit 1	X_1	Y_1
Observed unit 2	X_2	Y_2
	.	
	.	
	.	
Observed unit n	X_n	Y_n

Examples of data that would fit this pattern are people in a town (observed units) for each of whom we measure annual gross earnings (variable X) and the number of documented library visits per year (variable Y).

Or we might investigate the libraries in a region (observed units) and correlate their circulation activity (variable X) and their level of reader assistance (variable Y).

Or perhaps a librarian would want to study a sample of Zoology books (observed units) for the relationship between use (variable X) and number of illustrations (variable Y). It is important to note that in each case there are two observations for every observed unit. If this is not so, if there are not at least two observations per unit, a correlation study cannot be performed.

Another requirement for a correlation study is, of course, that the variables be functionally related to each other. There is little point in the correlation between the number of pages and the age in years of a sample of books unless there is reason to suspect some sort of cause and effect relationship between these two variables.

Also, the variables studied must be independent from each other. When two variables studied are merely two sides of the same coin, correlation means nothing. This can be demonstrated by an example. A few years ago a study was published in a library science journal. The investigator was looking for an answer to the question: are "in the library" use and "home" use of books associated? To this end data were collected that looked like these:

	X Number of books used in the library	Y Number of books used at home
Topic 1	100	50
Topic 2	80	70
		.
		.
		.
Topic n	X_n	Y_n

Clearly, these data look very much like pairs of observations made on a set of topics (observed units). For each topic we have a measure of "in the library" use and a measure of "home" use. The observations are clearly quantitative in nature. But are the variables independent from each other?

Let us take a close look at the data structure. The first of the two variables under study, X, is the number of instances of "in the library" use recorded for each topic during the period of the study. While we have no standard for judging whether this is good or bad we can certainly say that an X value of 100 is more than zero but less than the possible maximum we could have obtained.

The second of the two variables, Y, is the number of instances of "home" use recorded for the same topic. Here, too, a Y value of 50 is more than zero and less than the maximum possible.

The next question is, what are these maximum values? It would all depend on how many people use the library, on the accessibility of the books, maybe on the weather. The only firm value we can obtain is a count of the total number of recorded instances of use during the period studied. That total minus the number of recorded instances of "home" use is the maximum

possible value of "in the library" use. Likewise, the total of all uses minus
the number of recorded instances of "in the library" use is the maximum
possible value for "home use". What we have here are two variables, X and
Y, that are both functions of total use which we could name T. We can then
state this situation in equation form: $X + Y = T$. It follows that $T - X = Y$,
and that $T - Y = X$. In other words, if T is known and X is determined, then Y
is fixed. The variables X and Y, therefore, are not independent in this case.
What this means is that the correlation study was unnecessary since the
question is already answered from the start: of course the two variables
"in the library" use and "home" use are related. For as X increases so must
Y decrease since both are related to T!

In the field of library science data are notoriously difficult to conceptualize
and hard to measure. Researchers planning to perform correlation studies
must be especially on their guard to avoid the faux pas of correlating two things
that are not properly quantified; two things for which they do not have pairs of
observations; two things that are not functionally related; and two things that
are logical correlates of each other.

The calculations of correlation coefficients

The formulas for Pearson's r and Spearman's rho were already given. Since
there is quite a bit of computational labor involved in the calculations leading
to a correlation coefficient that even the investigator using a computer should
be cognizant of we present below a completely worked out example for each
of the two coefficients.

First, Pearson's product moment coefficient, r. To demonstrate the steps
in the computation of an r coefficient from simple ungrouped data let us consider
an entirely fictitious situation, one that was inspired, however, by an article
on scientific elitism that appeared in the <u>Journal of the American Society for
Information Science</u>. Let us say there were a theory that the more productive
thinkers in a field prefer literature-oriented methods of obtaining information
to person-oriented methods. As a consequence, we argue, the more productive
thinkers should also be the heaviest library users. To test this argument we
might reason that it should be possible to demonstrate that high productivity in
a sample of thinkers is positively correlated with intensity of library use.

An imaginary panel of peers selects those ten persons attached to a research
institute that are judged to be the most productive thinkers. For each of the ten
we obtain a measure of productivity (number of articles, reviews, books, and
patents published during the last five-year period). We also obtain a measure of
intensity of library use (number of recorded loan transactions during the same
period of time). The data thus collected might appear as shown in the
following tabulation:

	X Productivity	Y Intensity of library use
Thinker 1	20	1
Thinker 2	18	2
Thinker 3	15	12
Thinker 4	13	4
Thinker 5	12	5
Thinker 6	10	10
Thinker 7	8	11
Thinker 8	8	6
Thinker 9	6	16
Thinker 10	5	18

For these data an r coefficient is now to be computed. The formula for this coefficient was given before as

$$r = \frac{\Sigma xy}{\sqrt{\Sigma x^2 \times \Sigma y^2}}$$

This formula requires deviation scores, x and y, for its application, as well as their squares and their cross products. A key to the terms of the formula follows.

r : symbol for Pearson's correlation coefficient

xy : sum of the cross products of the deviation scores

x^2 : sum of the squared score deviations from the mean of the X distribution

y^2 : sum of the squared score deviations from the mean of the Y distribution

In order to apply the formula, therefore, we must begin by converting the raw observations into the required form. Here is a list of the steps involved:

Step 1:   Compute the mean for each distribution
($\overline{X}$ and $\overline{Y}$).

Step 2:   Compute the deviation scores by subtracting the
mean of the distribution from each of the raw
scores ($X - \overline{X} = x$; $Y - \overline{Y} = y$).

Step 3:   Multiply each x with its corresponding y to
obtain the cross product (xy).

Step 4:   Square each deviation score (x^2 and y^2).

Step 5:   Sum the cross products ($\sum xy$).

Step 6:   Sum the squared deviation scores ($\sum x^2$ and $\sum y^2$).

These operations have all been performed for the example:

Thinker	X	Y	x	y	xy	x^2	y^2
1	20	1	8.5	−7.5	−63.75	72.25	56.25
2	18	2	6.5	−6.5	−42.25	42.25	42.25
3	15	12	3.5	3.5	12.25	12.25	12.25
4	13	4	1.5	−4.5	−6.75	2.25	20.25
5	12	5	.5	−3.5	−1.75	.25	12.25
6	10	10	−1.5	1.5	−2.25	2.25	2.25
7	8	11	3.5	2.5	−8.75	12.25	6.25
8	8	6	−3.5	−2.5	8.75	12.25	6.25
9	6	16	−5.5	7.5	−41.25	30.25	56.25
10	5	18	−6.5	9.5	−61.75	42.25	90.25
Sums:	115	85			−207.5	228.5	304.5

$\overline{X} = 11.5$; $\overline{Y} = 8.5$; $N = 10$

Once the data have been transformed to deviations from the mean
the rest of the computation is easy. All one has to do is to substitute
the obtained sums in the formula:

$$r = \frac{\sum xy}{\sqrt{\sum x^2 \times \sum y^2}} = \frac{-207.5}{\sqrt{(228.5)(304.5)}} = \frac{-207.5}{263.7} = -.79$$

As it turns out, high productivity in our sample of thinkers is indeed highly correlated with intensity of library use (as the chart on page 77 explains, a coefficient of .79 indicates a substantial relationship), but negatively. In other words, the more productive a thinker, the fewer books he checks out for home use. The mathematical part of our study is clear and straightforward. This is what r=−.79 means, nothing more and nothing less. We could end here.

But it must be pointed out that the computation of a correlation coefficient should always be followed by an interpretation to extract its full meaning, and that this part of the job is more difficult than the computations. In our example, the negative correlation could mean at least two things. It could mean that our theory needs revision: the more productive thinkers in a field do not prefer literature-oriented methods of obtaining information to person-oriented methods. Or it might mean that our measure of library use was the wrong one. Maybe the theory is correct, but the more productive library users read their books in the library instead of checking them out for home use. The reader can probably think of several other possible interpretations. It is important to note that, while statistical methods are indispensable tools in library research, statistical methods will never yield the final decision. The interpretation of the results of any data analysis must be based on the purpose and design of the study. The determine "what it all means" at the end of a correlation study is an intuitive, creative, human activity. No amount of statistical or other mathematical manipulation of the data will take this responsibility from the researcher's shoulders.

But back to the computational work of correlation. Sometimes it is not desirable to calculate deviation scores and their squares, etc. It is possible to arrive at the same results using a different formula based on the original observations. One such formula reads as follows:

$$r = \frac{N\sum XY - (\sum X)(\sum Y)}{\sqrt{(N\sum X^2 - (\sum X)^2)(N\sum Y^2 - (\sum Y)^2)}}$$

Using the same data once more, here are the steps to be performed in the computation of r from original observations:

Step 1. Add the X and the Y scores to obtain their sums (ΣX and ΣY).

Step 2. Multiply each pair of scores to obtain their cross products (XY).

Step 3. Add the cross products (ΣXY).

Step 4. Square each score (X^2 and Y^2).

Step 5. Add the squared scores (ΣX^2 and ΣY^2)

Step 6. Square the sums of the scores ($(\Sigma X)^2$ and $(\Sigma Y)^2$).

All of these steps have been performed here:

X	Y	XY	X^2	Y^2
20	1	20	400	1
18	2	36	324	4
15	12	180	225	144
13	4	52	169	16
12	5	60	144	25
10	10	100	100	100
8	11	88	64	121
8	6	48	64	36
6	16	96	36	256
5	18	90	25	384
Sums: 115	85	770	1551	1027

$(\Sigma X)^2 = 13,225$

$(\Sigma Y)^2 = 7,225$

At the bottom of the table we find all the sums we need. Substituting the values in the formula we have:

$$r = \frac{N\sum XY - (\sum X)(\sum Y)}{\sqrt{(N\sum X^2 - (\sum X)^2)(N\sum Y^2 - (\sum Y)^2)}}$$

$$= \frac{10(770) - (115)(85)}{\sqrt{(10(1551) - 13225)(10(1027) - 7225)}}$$

$$= \frac{-2075}{2636}$$

$$= -.79$$

As the reader can see, the alternative computational formula leads to the same result.

Now for the computation of a rho coefficient. The formula was already given on page 78:

$$r_S = 1 - \frac{6\sum d^2}{N^3 - N}$$

Here is a key to the symbols employed:

r_S : symbol for Spearman's rank rorrelation coefficient rho

d^2 : sum of the squared differences between the ranks of the pairs of variables

N : number of pairs of observations

Let us say that in an attempt to find a valid way of screening applicants for employment as library technical assistants a library director reasons that clerical work in technical processing requires aptitudes similar to those required for work in data processing. If this were true, he deduces, performance on a data processing aptitude test should be strongly related to job performance as a technical assistant.

By a stroke of luck he finds ten library technical assistants who have been rated successful by their respective employers. Each of the ten had taken a data processing aptitude test before being hired, and the scores obtained by each person are available. To quantify the employers' judgements, ratings on a home-made LTA effectiveness scale are obtained for each of the ten:

	X Data processing aptitude scores	Y LTS effectiveness scores
Assistant 1	30	30
Assistant 2	35	20
Assistant 3	40	25
Assistant 4	50	50
Assistant 5	60	80
Assistant 6	75	40
Assistant 7	80	60
Assistant 8	90	55
Assistant 9	92	95
Assistant 10	99	90

As was explained before, rankings on a scale can be conveniently compared by means of Spearman's rho. This coefficient is based on data in the form of ranks. Here are the steps needed to convert the raw scores to ranks:

Step 1. Convert the scores in both variables to ranks

Step 2. Find the difference in each pair of ranks (d)

Step 3. Square the differences (d^2)

Step 4. Sum the squared differences ($\sum d^2$)

These operations have been performed for the example:

	X	Rank	Y	Rank	d	d^2
Ass't 1	30	1	30	3	-2	4
Ass't 2	35	2	20	1	1	1
Ass't 3	40	3	25	2	1	1
Ass't 4	50	4	50	5	-1	1
Ass't 5	60	5	80	8	-3	9
Ass't 6	75	6	40	4	2	4
Ass't 7	80	7	60	7	0	0
Ass't 8	90	8	55	6	2	4
Ass't 9	92	9	95	10	-1	1
Ass't 10	99	10	90	9	1	1

$$\sum d^2 = 26$$

The rest of the work is very easy. One simply substitutes the values from the table in the formula:

$$r_S = 1 - \frac{6\sum d^2}{N^3 - N} = 1 - \frac{156}{990} = 1 - .16 = .84$$

The result strengthens the library director's theory that performance on the data processing aptitude test can be used to predict performance of library technical assistants. A look at the table on page 77 confirms that a coefficient of .84 indicates a strong correlation between the two variables.

The examples given in this chapter were all trivial and based on samples of ten observed units each to keep the demonstration simple. Real data in a correlation study will consist of large numbers of pairs of observations and the computational work involved will become progressively more cumbersome. With improved access to computers -- even high schools and junior colleges have time sharing terminals for their students nowadays -- library researchers will find it easier to perform serious correlational work by machine. The interested reader should turn to Appendix 1 for suggestions on how to go about this.

10. REGRESSION AND TIME SERIES

A hypothetical library buys approximately one hundred books every Monday. The staff manages to process from seventy to ninety of these by Friday, adding every week an average of twenty books to the backlog of unprocessed books. This has been going on, let us say, for twenty weeks, and due to a freeze on hiring and several other regulations nothing can be done to change this situation for another thirty-two weeks at least. The librarian wishes to estimate what the total backlog will be at the end of the fifty-two week period.

He can express the relationship between the backlog of unprocessed books and the number of weeks elapsed in terms of a mathematical equation such as the one that follows:

$$B = (A - P) W$$

where B stands for backlog, W is the number of weeks in question, A is the weekly acquisitions rate, and P is the weekly processing rate. The weekly backlog of unprocessed books is, obviously, the weekly acquisitions rate (100) less the amount processed (80). If this backlog is allowed to accumulate for fifty-two weeks the total backlog after this period, our formula says, can be predicted to be

$$B = (100-80)(52) = 1040 \text{ books}$$

Armed with such a equation the librarian can estimate the size of the backlog for any given period of weeks. As long as A and P remain constant the value of B can be calculated for any given value of W. Thus, for W=63 weeks, the backlog would be predicted to come to

$$B = (100-80)(63) = 1260 \text{ books}$$

Many decisions in the library world are made on the basis of such reasoning which could, if one wanted to go to the trouble, be expressed by equations. Often, this is not necessary. But there is one particular equation that is so well suited for describing certain relationships between phenomena that it has become a standard in the repertoire of descriptive statistics, and that is the equation for the straight line, $Y = a+bX$.

It is also called the linear equation because the plot of all the values of X and Y that satisfy this equation forms a straight line. That this is so is best demonstrated by an example. Let us assume we had two constants, a=1, and b=2.5. Let us further assume we had four values of X: 2,4,6,and 8. Using the linear equation we can calculate from these data the value of Y that corresponds to each of the four X values, as is shown in the following table:

X	2	4	6	8
Y (a + bX)	6	11	16	21

If we plot the points corresponding to these four pairs of values on ordinary graph paper we obtain four points that lie on a straight line:

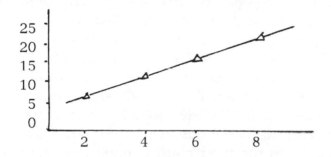

Once this linear relationship between any two sets of data is established the equation can be used for predicting or estimating other values of Y from given values of X. In the foregoing example, if X were 3 and a and b remained constant, Y can be predicted to be equal to 1+2.5(3) = 8.5. For an X of 7 we obtain a Y of 1+2.5(7)=18.5, and so on. Because the equation can be used in this way it is often referred to as the estimating equation.

Now, of course, the coordinates of pairs of related data in the real world rarely if ever fall exactly on a straight line. But often they approximate a linear distribution and the linear equation can be used to fit a straight line to the data. Or, said differently, given some observations, the estimating equation can be used to estimate missing values of the dependent variable. This is also known as curve fitting.

We can explain practical curve fitting methods best by means of another example. Let us say we had reason to believe that two phenomena of library operations were related as shown by this hypothetical plot:

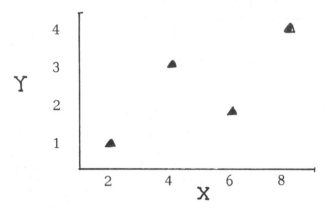

The object is to construct the one straight line that fits these data best. This requires an answer to the question "what is best?". We shall answer the question by adopting the so-called least squares criterion: that line is considered to fit the data best for which the sum of the squares of the distances from all observations, taken parallel to the Y axis, is a minimum.

Here is the same plot again. We have added two straight lines, K and L, which both seem to fit the data well. But when we construct the distance from the first point to each line and actually draw in the squares we see that the square of the distance from P_1 to line L is much smaller than that of the distance from P_1 to line K.

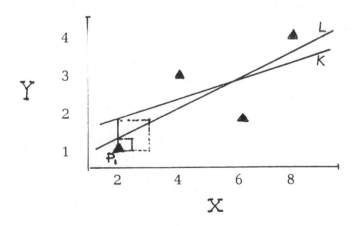

93

If we could draw in the rest of the squares and compare the sums we would see that the sum of the squares for line L is considerably smaller than that for line K. In fact, it can be shown mathematically that there is one line, and one line only, for which this sum is less than for any other conceivable line we could draw to fit these data. This line is the least squares line of best fit, in our example, line L.

Our least squares line, we observe, has a certain slope to it. This slope represents a measure of increase in Y units for every unit increase in X. In our earlier example we had a constant b = 2.5, which meant that every time X increased by a unit, we observed an increase of 2.5 units in the Y variable. When X was 2, for example, Y was 6. If we had taken X as 3 instead, Y would have increased by 2.5 units, or 6+2.5 =8.5. The visible slope in the plot, then, corresponds to the constant b in the equation presented on 90: Y = a + bX.

For completeness' sake we must say that the constant a in the equation corresponds to that point on the plot where the line intercepts the Y axis. This is of no practical significance in this context. But once we have defined the a and the b coefficients we can easily reason our way to the conclusion that for any set of bivariate observations that can be assumed to be approximately linearly related we can calculate the value of Y for any given value of X by simply computing these two constants, the intercept a and the slope b. This is the essence of regression analysis.

The computation of a and b involves the methods of differential calculus which lead to the establishment of two normal equations. When solved simultaneously, these normal equations yield the desired values of a and b. Here is a way to reason how these normal equations come into being without going through the process of differentiation. If we wish to estimate just one point, Y_e, we can express this operation by means of the linear equation:

$$Y_e = a + bX$$

If there are many points we must sum up all terms:

$$\sum Y = \sum a + b \sum X$$

Since $\sum a$ is the same thing as Na we can write this first normal equation in this way:

$$\sum Y = Na + b \sum X$$

Now for the second normal equation. We begin with the simple linear equation, Y = a + bX. This time we multiply each term by the coefficient of b, which is X. (Since the coefficient of a was 1 we did not have to do this step for the first normal equation). After this multiplication by X we have the following equation:

$$YX = aX + bX^2$$

Since we want the equation to cover all observations we must sum over all N values again, which gives this equation:

$$\Sigma YX = a\Sigma X + b\Sigma X^2$$

This is the second normal equation.

We are now ready to put the data from our example into the equations. Here are the data in tabulated form:

X	Y	X^2	YX
2	1	4	2
4	3	16	12
6	2	36	12
8	4	64	32
20	10	120	58

Into the first normal equation we now substitute the approriate data from the example:

$$\Sigma Y = Na + b\Sigma X$$

$$10 = 4a + 20b$$

And into the second equation we put the requisite data as follows:

$$\Sigma YX = a\Sigma X + b\Sigma X^2$$

$$58 = 20a + 120b$$

To solve these two equations simultaneously for b we multiply the first by 5.

This yields the following equation:

$$50 = 20a + b(100)$$

We can now subtract this first equation from the second:

$$58 = 20a + b(120)$$
$$-\quad\underline{50 = 20a + b(100)}$$
$$8 = \qquad\quad b(20)$$

After this operation we can divide both sides of the resulting equation by 20 and solve for b:

$$b = \frac{8}{20} = .4$$

The value for a is obtained when we substitute all our known values in the original first equation and solve for a:

$$10 = 4a + (.4)(20)$$
$$4a = 10 - 8$$
$$a = 2/4 = .5$$

Since a straight line is defined when two of its points are given, we can very simply check out line L of our example. Let us calculate the least squares Y values corresponding to an X of 2 and an X of 8, respectively. We use the estimating equation Y = a + bX and substitute the known values to obtain

$$Y_1 = .5 + (.4)(2) = 1.3$$

and

$$Y_2 = .5 + (.4)(8) = 3.7$$

Here is the plot once more showing the two computed points Y_1 and Y_2:

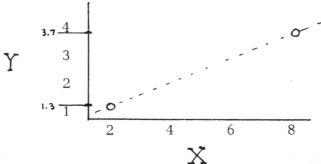

Undoubtedly there are innumerable situations in the library world where a knowledge of the relation between two variables is of great interest to a researcher or administrator. For purposes of demonstration or planning, particularly, the methodology of regression analysis is therefore potentially of great usefulness to librarians. But regression analysis is based on bivariate data, observations made on two variables that are both measurable, and such data are rare in the library field. We can measure a book, true enough. We can take its height, weigh it, count the number of pages, or establish its cost in dollars. But this is very seldom what we need to know to solve library problems or make relevant predictions. Instead, we are more likely to be interested in the quality of the book, its popularity, the adequacy of its catalog description, or similar information that is not directly obtainable by measurement. And as long as we are interested in variables that cannot be expressed as quantities, quantitative methods such as regression analysis do not help us as much as we might wish.

There is, however, a class of problems that is of the greatest practical importance in the library field, especially in administrative and evaluative work: time series analysis. Time series analysis, or in a narrower sense, trend analysis, utilizes the methodology of regression analysis. There is one difference. In trend analysis problems we deal with data that consist of observations on one variable only, made during longer periods of time. Examples of such data collected over time are annual acquisitions or expenditures over the last twenty years; fines collected per week for the last 104 weeks; monthly circulation figures for the most recent 36-month period. Such data are said to constitute time series. They can be plotted on a coordinate system in which the time periods are shown along the X axis. Here is an example. Let us say we had collected these data:

Year	Volumes acquired	Year	Volumes acquired
1956	4,000	1966	7,000
1957	3,000	1967	8,000
1958	5,000	1968	9,000
1959	8,000	1969	9,000
1960	9,000	1970	5,000
1961	5,000	1971	10,000
1962	10,000	1972	6,000
1963	7,000	1973	9,000
1964	5,000	1974	8,000
1965	7,000		

These data can be plotted as follows:

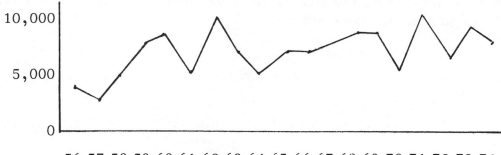

The plotted points form a zig-zag curve that is far from a straight line. Yet it is undeniable that, on the whole, there seems to be an upward trend in these data. Using the regression equation we can compute the line of best fit for this set of coordinates as for any other set of linearly related points.

Since in a time series the X variable represents a series of successive time periods (years, months, weeks, or perhaps days), i.e. a series of equal units, the computation can be greatly simplified by re-coding the X variable around a zero origin in the middle of the scale.

The series of nineteen years from 1956 to 1974, for example, can be re-coded as follows:

Year	Coded
1956	−9
1957	−8
1958	−7
1959	−6
1960	−5
1961	−4
1962	−3
1963	−2
1964	−1
1965	0
1966	1
1967	2
1968	3
1969	4
1970	5
1971	6
1972	7
1973	8
1974	9

When we treat the years as numbers (left column) their sum comes to
37335. After coding the sum reduces to zero! This simplifies procedures
greatly because when the sum of the X variates is reduced to zero the first
normal equation becomes simply

$$\sum Y = Na$$

From this we can derive a simple formula for the calculation of the
a constant:

$$a = \frac{\sum Y}{N}$$

By a similar procedure we find that the computation of the b constant
is also simplified. When the sum of X is zero, the second normal
equation becomes simply

$$\sum XY = b\sum x^2$$

From this we derive a formula for the computation of b:

$$b = \frac{\sum YX}{\sum x^2}$$

As a result of these simplifications we are enabled to calculate the
trend line for the data of page 97 with a minimum of computational
work. Here are the necessary steps. First the sums required for the
a and b formulas must be assembled ($\sum Y$, $\sum XY$, and $\sum x^2$).

X	Y	XY	x^2	X	Y	XY	x^2
−9	4	−36	81	1	7	7	1
−8	3	−24	64	2	8	16	4
−7	5	−35	49	3	9	27	9
−6	8	−48	36	4	9	36	16
−5	9	−45	25	5	5	25	25
−4	5	−20	16	6	10	60	36
−3	10	−30	9	7	6	42	49
−2	7	−14	4	8	9	72	64
−1	5	− 5	1	9	8	72	81
0	7	0	0		134	100	570

From the assembled sums the a coefficient is easily determined:

$$a = \frac{\Sigma Y}{N} = \frac{134}{19} = 7.05$$

The b coefficient can be computed as follows:

$$b = \frac{\Sigma YX}{\Sigma X^2} = \frac{100}{570} = .18$$

Now the trend line is constructed. Two points are needed to fix a straight line on a plane. We arbitrarily pick two years such as 1961 (-4) and 1971 (+6):

$$Y_{1961} = a + bX = 7.05 + .18(-4) = 6.33 \text{ thousand}$$

$$Y_{1971} = 7.05 + .18(6) = 8.13 \text{ thousand}$$

When we plot the two resulting points on a graph and connect them by a straight line, we get the trend line for our data. The graph is shown here again, with the calculated trend line superimposed on the original observations:

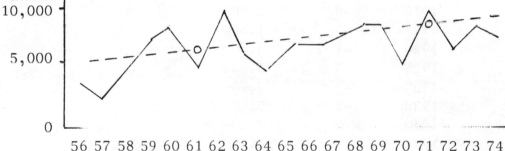

Such a line can be very useful for demonstrating a historical trend. A librarian might use it to advantage in an annual report, for example.

The trend line, or the equation on which it is based, is often used for planning or forecasting purposes. From a strictly mathematical point of view this is a questionable procedure. Observing the past gives us no knowledge of the future. We can make valid statements only about the range of data for which we have observations, in the example used, some acquisitions data from 1956 to 1974. All predictions beyond 1974 are risky. Yet in research and administration as in life forecasts on the basis of past performance are very common.

To continue with the same example, let us say our librarian was interested in predicting his probable acquisitions rate three years hence. He can simply extend the line in the graph toward the right and read off the approximate Y value corresponding to the X value of 1977, coded 12.

A more precise value can be calculated by means of the estimating equation, as follows:

$$Y_{1977} = 7.05 + .18(12) = 9.21 \text{ thousand}$$

The Y value obtained is the estimated acquisition rate in thousands of volumes for the year 1977. The reader must be warned, however, that this forecast presupposes a continuation of the past trend, which is pure conjecture on the part of the forecaster.

The linear trend is certainly a very useful technique for work with time series. But in the real world we often encounter data that show nonlinear trends, and they require slightly different methods for their description and for planning and forecasting purposes. Let us consider another set of fictitious data, annual book production statistics for a span of sixty years:

Year	Coded	Annual book production
1910	−6	2,000
1915	−5	1,500
1920	−4	3,000
1925	−3	3,500
1930	−2	3,750
1935	−1	5,000
1940	0	8,000
1945	1	6,500
1950	2	10,000
1955	3	12,000
1960	4	16,000
1965	5	17,000
1970	6	23,000

When these data are plotted it becomes apparent that, while there is a definite upward trend, this trend is not linear but parabolic:

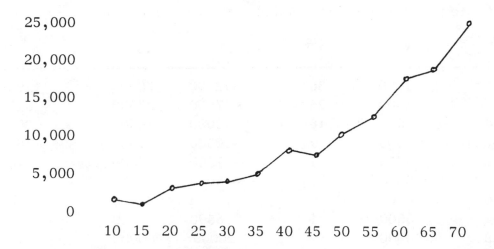

A parabola is described by the second degree equation:

$$Y = a + bX + cX^2$$

Work with this equation involves the computation of three coefficients or constants, a, b, and c. Instead of two normal equations we need three. The first normal equation is found when we multiply each term by the coefficient of a and sum over all observations:

$$\Sigma Y = Na + b\Sigma X + c\Sigma X^2$$

The second normal equation results when we multiply by the coefficient of b and sum:

$$\Sigma YX = a\Sigma X + b\Sigma X^2 + c\Sigma X^3$$

And the third equation is the result of multiplying by the coefficient of c, and summing:

$$\Sigma YX^2 = a\Sigma X^2 + b\Sigma X^3 + c\Sigma X^4$$

When the X variable, time, is coded from -6 to $+6$ as we have done on page 100, the sum of X and the sum of X^3 become zero. This simplifies the first normal equation to read:

$$\Sigma Y = Na + c\Sigma X^2$$

102

The second normal equation becomes $\sum YX = b\sum X^2$, and the third,

$$\sum YX^2 = a\sum X^2 + c\sum X^4.$$

In order to proceed we must assemble the necessary sums:

X	Y	X^2	YX	YX^2	X^4
−6	2000	36	−12000	72000	1296
−5	1500	25	− 7500	37500	625
−4	3000	16	−12000	48000	256
−3	3500	9	−10500	31500	81
−2	3750	4	− 7500	15000	16
−1	5000	1	− 5000	5000	1
0	8000	0	0	0	0
1	6500	1	6500	6500	1
2	10000	4	20000	40000	16
3	12000	9	36000	108000	81
4	16000	16	64000	256000	256
5	17000	25	85000	425000	625
6	23000	36	138000	828000	1296
	111250	182	295000	1872500	4550

When we substitute the appropriate sums in the second equation we obtain a value for b as follows:

$$b = \frac{295000}{182} = 1620.88$$

To compute the values for a and c we solve the first and the third equations simultaneously, as follows. First, we substitute the appropriate data in the first equation:

$$111250 = 13a + 182c$$

For the third equation we obtain:

$$1872500 = 182a + 4550c$$

If we divide the third equation by 14 we obtain

$$133750 = 13a + 325c$$

And if we now subtract the first equation from the third we get this:

$$133750 = 13a + 325c$$
$$- \quad 111250 = 13a + 182c$$

$$22500 = \qquad 143c$$

Solving for c we get

$$c = \frac{22500}{143} = 157.34$$

Finally, we find the a coefficient by substituting b and c in the first equation:

$$133750 = 13a + 182(157.34)$$
$$a = \frac{82613.5}{13}$$
$$a = 8085.7$$

Armed with these three constants,

$$a = 8085.7$$
$$b = 1620.88$$
$$c = 157.34$$

we can easily forecast the expected book production rate for, say, 1985 (coded 9):

$$Y_{1985} = 8085.7 + (1620.88)(9) + (157.34)(81)$$

$$= 35418 \text{ volumes.}$$

Had we used the linear equation instead of the parabolic our forecast would have been

$$Y_{1985} = a + bX$$
$$= 8557.69 + 1620.88(9)$$
$$= 23145 \text{ volumes.}$$

The difference comes to 12273 volumes, and in real life a difference of this magnitude may well spoil a planning effort. This may serve as a warning, then. It is of the greatest importance that the librarian be certain of the nature of the trend -- linear or non-linear -- before undertaking a trend analysis.

INFERENTIAL STATISTICS

11. THE NORMAL CURVE
AND
CONFIDENCE INTERVALS

If the world of libraries were full of certainties and easily observed variables, any research project would simply consist of two steps: a problem statement and a design to collect the relevant data. One would merely gather the requisite information and watch all the facts emerge. In reality, of course, library science is full of uncertainties. And variables in the field are seldom as easily measured as we should wish. Furthermore, the facts librarians collect are practically never based on the total population of relevant cases. Instead, the library field shares with other fields of human endeavour the necessity of basing most decisions on data collected from relatively small samples. But, while data collected from a sample are an accurate representation of that sample, they are not necessarily representative of the entire population from which the sample was chosen.

Therefore, whenever we study a phenomenon on the basis of a sample we must recognize that our findings necessarily deviate somewhat from the whole truth. One can never learn all the facts about a population phenomenon from the study of a sample. It is possible to eliminate many factors and variables, but in the end one is always left with uncertainty. There is no remedy against this. But that does not mean that librarians have to abandon all research efforts. Instead, if we interpret "research" as the process of scientific inquiry that proceeds from uncertainty to a state of -- not certainty, that is probably unattainable for humans --but relatively greater certainty, we shall have built the first half of the bridge we need to get over this river of uncertainty.

How can we build the rest of the bridge? How can we take the results of an admittedly inadequate sample and arrive at a statement of relative certainty about a phenomenon of the real world? How can we bridge this gap between the limited information we have and the total we need for a reasonably certain decision? The missing element in the bridge is a model of the real world. If a model can be found that accurately represents the phenomenon under investigation, then sample findings can be interpreted in terms of that model and statements about the phenomenon can be made, including statements about the degree of certainty involved. This is the essence of inferential statistics, and the model most often used is the normal curve.

The normal curve, also called the Gaussian or normal distribution, is a model for many actual populations. It is the distribution characteristic for all chance generated events that occur in large numbers. The model dates back some two hundred years to the French mathematician Abraham De Moivre who developed its equation. The nature of this distribution can be visualized very clearly by a little experiment with three pennies.

A penny can be seen as an apparatus that has two states: it can rest either head up, or tail up. Thus, if a penny is flipped it must come down as a head (H) or as a tail (T). No other outcomes are possible if we disallow the rare chance of a penny landing on edge. Since there are only two outcomes, we can reason that the probability of a random toss resulting in a head (H) is p = .5.

The same probability attaches to the other outcome, T. Its probability is q = .5.

What this means is that if we tossed the penny a large number of times, say one thousand times, chances are that it would come up H about five hundred times.

Now to our three penny experiment. If we toss all three pennies at once we have no way to know how they will come down -- all heads? all tails? or a combination of both? But we can say one thing with absolute certainty, namely, that the three pennies can come to rest in only one of eight combinations, no more and no less. Here are the eight possible outcomes:

HHH	HTT
HHT	THT
HTH	TTH
THH	TTT

We saw that the probability of one penny coming down H was p = .5. De Moivre saw that the combined probabilities of three binomial events like these were equal to $p \times p \times p = p^3$. In our experiment this means that the probability of the first outcome, HHH, is equal to

$$p = .5^3 = .125$$

What would be the probability of the second outcome, HHT? Simply this:

$$p \times p \times q = .5^3 = .125$$

As a matter of fact, we will find that all eight outcomes have the same probability, .125. We can now present all this in a table for clarity:

	Outcome	Probability		
1.	HHH	p^3	=	.125
2.	HHT	p^2q	=	.125
3.	HTH	p^2q	=	.125
4.	THH	p^2q	=	.125
5.	HTT	pq^2	=	.125
6.	THT	pq^2	=	.125
7.	TTH	pq^2	=	.125
8.	TTT	q^3	=	.125
Total				1.000

Notice that the sum of the probabilities is 1 or unity, which confirms that there are no more than eight possible outcomes. Also notice that this experiment of tossing three pennies can be described as raising a binomial event $(p+q)$ to the third power, as expanding the binomial to the third, an operation defined by the following equation:

$$(p + q)^3 = p^3 + 3p^2q + 3pq^2 + q^3$$

A look at the table will confirm that this is exactly what we have done.

We can easily imagine what would happen if we tossed four pennies instead of three. We should simply raise the binomial to the fourth:

$$(p + q)^4 = p^4 + 4p^3q + 6p^2q^2 + 4pq^3 + q^4$$

Apart from furnishing an interesting diversion, these considerations have a very practical side. Let us again use a picture to demonstrate. In the following tabulation we show the sixteen possible outcomes of tossing four pennies, with their associated probabilities. In addition to that we have grouped like outcomes together since we do not really care which particular penny came up H or T. All we are interested in is the total number of H and T outcomes in each throw of four pennies. And finally, we have shown graphically by little squares how the probabilities "stack up" for each group. Here is the tabulation:

Outcome		Probability	
Group I four heads	HHHH	.0625	□
Group II three heads	HHHT	.0625	
	HHTH	.0625	
	HTHH	.0625	□ □ □ □
	THHH	.0625	
Group III two heads	HHTT	.0625	
	HTHT	.0625	
	THTH	.0625	
	HTTH	.0625	□ □ □ □ □ □
	TTHH	.0625	
	THHT	.0625	
Group IV one head	TTTH	.0625	
	TTHT	.0625	
	THTT	.0625	□ □ □ □
	HTTT	.0625	
Group V no heads	TTTT	.0625	□

The tabulation shows that the middle outcome (two heads) is likely to occur most often, and that the extremes (all heads or all tails) are bound to happen relatively seldom in any given number of tosses. If we now turn the picture of the stacked squares sideways, we obtain this model

110

All we need to do is to connect the tops of the squares by a smooth curved line and we obtain a fine approximation of the graph of the normal distribution:

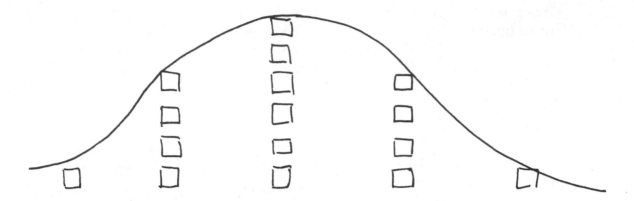

This, of course, is the model we are looking for, the normal curve.

The normal curve is strictly a theoretical model describing the outcomes of any large number of binomial, or chance, events. This model has some interesting properties. For example, it can be said to be a standard geometrical shape. What does this mean? Take a square, for example. A square is another standard geometrical shape. Draw the diagonal

We know instinctively, and a mathematician could prove it to us, that in this standard geometrical shape the diagonal divides the total area into two exactly equivalent portions. The shape is said to be "standard" because it has this same property regardless of its size. Compare these two squares:

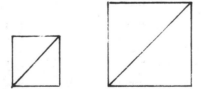

The diagonal cuts both exactly in half. This is true for all squares.

The normal curve is also a standard shape. If we erect an ordinate at the mean of the distribution,

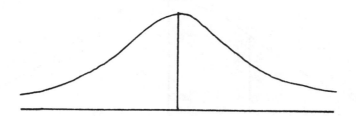

we can be certain that this ordinate cuts the total area under the curve exactly into two halves. Said differently, one of the interesting and useful properties of our model is the fact that fifty per cent of the area under the curve lie on either side of the ordinate erected at the mean. The mean of the normal distribution can be seen as the balancing point. The weight of all the scores on one side of it is equal to that of the scores on the other side. Mathematically, we say that the mean of our model is zero, or $\mu = 0$. Its standard deviation is unity, or $\sigma = 1$.

Let us return for a moment to the simpler shape of the square. If we drew both diagonals instead of one we would obtain this picture:

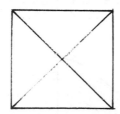

If we designate the total area within this square as 1 we can easily see that the area in each of the triangles created by the two diagonals must be ¼ of the total, or .25. The square being a standard shape, this relationship holds for all squares.

The area under the normal curve can be treated similarly. Let us mark off a few points on the base line:

-2σ -1σ $\mu = 0$ 1σ 2σ

If we superimpose the curve onto this line and erect ordinates at the five points marked off, we obtain this picture:

112

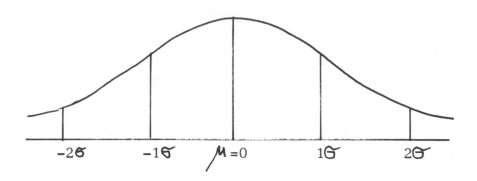

Although it looks quite different, this shape is analogous to the
square with the two diagonals. We know precisely what proportion
of the total area under the curve is found between any two ordinates.
Between the ordinates erected at the mean and the one erected one
standard deviation on one side of it we find .3413 of the total area.
Or, said differently, about 68 per cent of the area under the normal
curve lie between the ordinates erected one standard deviation out
from the mean. The other areas are also known. We present them
in the following illustration:

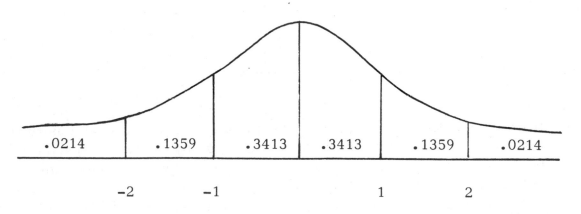

If we extended the markings to 3σ, 4σ, and so on, we would
find that the corresponding areas diminish rapidly. However,
theoretically the curve never touches the base line. It is an
asymptotic curve. This property need not concern us, however, since
most of our work with the model will be confined to the portion between
the mean and the ordinates erected 3σ out, an area that includes
more than 99 per cent of the total area under the curve.

But how can we expect this theoretical model of a population to serve as a bridge between the limited data we may have collected and the real truth? Figuratively, one could say that this is done by stretching what-ever data we have upon the model as one stretches a 3-inch rubber band to fit a 6-inch stack of catalog cards.

Supposing we had determined by a careful study that the average library user in town checks out twelve books per year ($\mu = 12$). We have also determined that this distribution of checkout rates has a standard deviation of three books ($\sigma = 3$). For purposes of a bond issue election prognosti-cation we need to have the opinion of a typical library user. We go out and randomly pick one gentleman from the crowd. In the course of the ensuing interview we learn that this gentleman is a library user, and that he checks out at least twenty books each year. The question arises, how typical is this user?

Obviously, there is no way for us to be certain. We could guess and say that our sample of one is probably fairly typical, or some such thing. But we can do much better if we utilize the model of the normal curve. To do this we must convert our observation into the terms of the standard normal curve. This transformation can be done in two steps. First, we convert our observed score (20 books) into a deviation score by subtracting from it the mean of the distribution (12 books). Next, we convert that deviation score into a standard score, or z score, as it is often called, by dividing it by its standard deviation (3 books). Here are the two steps in a diagram:

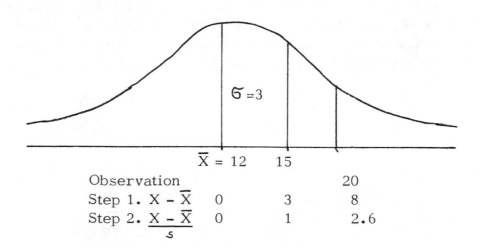

	$\bar{X} = 12$	15	
Observation			20
Step 1. $X - \bar{X}$	0	3	8
Step 2. $\dfrac{X - \bar{X}}{s}$	0	1	2.6

The curve represents the population of users. In step 1 we have shown the deviation scores for all three values, 12 − 12, 15 − 12, and 20 − 12. In step 2 we have computed the z scores. We interpret the results as follows.

Having stretched our one observation over the model, so to say, we find that X = 20 corresponds to a standard score z = 2.6. Since the area beyond a given ordinate in the model can be intepreted either as a proportion or as a probability -- we recall that the curve was based on probabilities of occurrences of certain chance events -- we can now say in terms of the model that the probability of picking a 20-book user at random from this population is equal to the area to the right of the ordinate erected at σ = 2.6. Graphically, this is the situation:

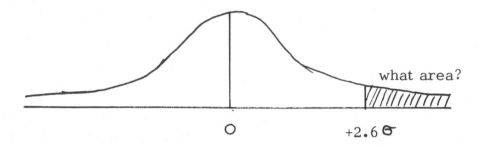

We want to know the magnitude of the area in the shaded portion under the curve. Table C in Appendix 5 reveals that the area of the normal curve to the right of the ordinate erected at z = 2.6 is .0047. Translated into terms of our problem this amounts to saying that the man we selected was a very untypical user indeed: less than one half of one per cent (.0047) of the users in this town check out as many books per year as he did!

Here is another example. Let us say we had data on a population of 500 librarians. Their salaries were recorded and the mean was computed as μ = 14,000 dollars. The standard deviation came to σ= 2,500 dollars. Let us say the question had arisen how many of the 500 librarians earn more than 17,000 dollars. Whithout having to go back to the original data, we can arrive at the answer in a few steps, as follows. Let the curve pictured below stand for the population of 500 librarians:

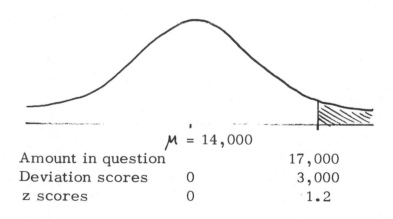

	μ = 14,000	
Amount in question		17,000
Deviation scores	0	3,000
z scores	0	1.2

We find that the value inquestion, 17,000 dolars, corresponds to a
z score of +1.2. Turning to table C at z = 1.2 we read an area of
11.5 per cent. We can interpret this value as follows: about 12 per cent
earn 17,000 or more, or, in numbers,

$$\frac{500 \times 12}{100} = 60 \text{ librarians}$$

Incidentally, had we asked how many earn less than 11,000 dollars,
we should have found the same percentage. The computation is as
follows:

deviation score: –3,000 dollars
z score: –1.2

The model is symmetric. Hence the proportions for a given z are the
same regardless of the sign. In our case, we should have concluded
that about 12 per cent, or 60 librarians, earn 11,000 dollars or less.

Many tables of the normal curve give areas and z values for both, one-
tail and two-tail problems. Here is a simplified table of this kind.

Area (%)	z (one-tail)	z (two-tail)
50	0	0.67
10	1.28	1.65
5	1.65	1.96
1	2.33	2.57

Concepts like this are often easier to grasp when visualized graphically.
Here is a curve showing 50 per cent of the area all in one tail:

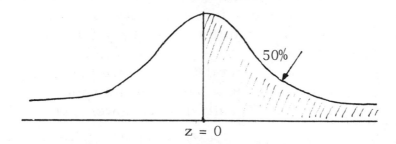

z = 0

Obviously this situation occurs only when z is equal to 0, as the one-tail
table shows. Now let us look at a curve where 50 per cent of the area
are left in both tails:

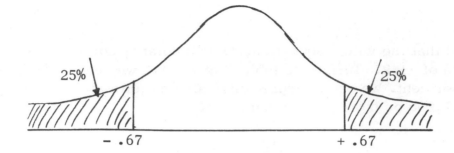

25%   25%

− .67   + .67

This happens when +z and −z have the same absolute value of .67.

Here is a fictitious problem for practice with the two-tail table. A survey divulged that there were 1,001 libraries of a certain kind in a country. Their mean holdings in volumes was 68,000. The standard deviation came to 15,000 volumes. Let us assume that the question now was, where are the middle 90 per cent of this population located? Between which two volume counts will we find 9/10 of the libraries? The problem can be diagrammed like this:

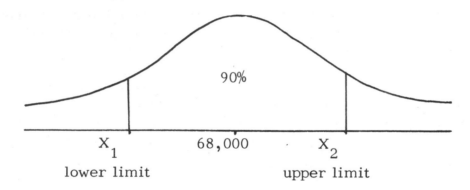

90%

X_1 68,000 X_2

lower limit   upper limit

If 90 per cent of the libraries straddle the mean this requires that 10 per cent are outside this middle group, in terms of volume counts. Since the curve is symmetrical, we know that we shall find 10/2 or 5 per cent in either tail. A look at our two-tail table tells us that this happens whenever z equals 1.65. Or said differently, at z = ± 1.65, 10 per cent of the area under the normal curve are in both tails.

To finish with the problem we must collect data. We have the mean of the distribution, 68,000 volumes. We know the desired z value (± 1.65). We can now solve for X_1 and X_2, the desired lower and upper limits. We know that z is equal to $X - \mu/\sigma$. Substituting the known values in the equation we get the lower values as follows:

$$-1.65 = \frac{X_1 - 68,000}{15,000}$$

$$X_1 = 68,000 + (-1.65) \times 15,000$$

$$= 68,000 + (-24,750)$$

$$= 43,250 \text{ volumes.}$$

Similarly, the upper value comes to

$$X_2 = 68,000 + (1.65) \text{ X } 15,000$$

$$= 68,000 + 24,750$$

$$= 92,750 \text{ volumes.}$$

The answer to the question now emerges: 90 per cent of the libraries in the population surveyed have between 43,250 and 92,750 volumes in their collections.

It should be noted that the model of the normal curve is suitable only for data that can be considered chance generated. Bibliographic data like those used in the last example are often non-normally distributed. It is obviously not true that most libraries are middle sized while a few are small and a few are large, which would be the characteristic of a normal distribution. Instead, most libraries are small, a few are middle sized, and very few are large. The log-normal distribution curve of holdings of United States academic libraries, for example, was plotted by Pratt in Library Quarterly for July 1975 approximately as follows:

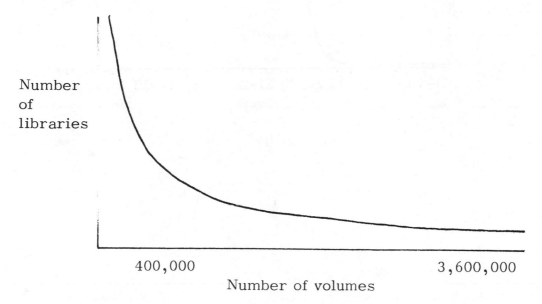

118

Many other phenomena in life are not normally distributed. Take, for example, a group of college students. Most will be young; few will be of retirement age; and there will be no infants at all. When plotted, the age distribution of college students will not resemble the normal curve. Instead it will look like this:

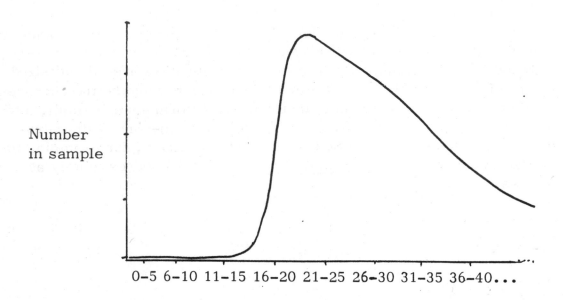

Number
in sample

0-5 6-10 11-15 16-20 21-25 26-30 31-35 36-40...

Age

Several other non-normal distributions are possible for which standard statistical procedures are not appropriate. At this writing, however, no definitive treatise of inferential statistics for non-normally distributed bibliometric and library data has been published. In this chapter, therefore, we continue to assume an underlying normal distribution in all data. In other chapters we shall work with the chi square distribution, the t distribution, and the F distribution.

Practical problems in library science will seldom be solved by discussions of the properties of whole populations. Instead, investigators will normally deal with samples drawn either from populations that are finite, such as all public libraries serving United States cities of 100,000 inhabitants or more, or from imaginary populations such as all past, present, and future library users of a certain kind. The basic considerations remain the same. The investigator must stretch his sample data over a suitable population model in order to say how close he thinks he has come to the truth, how certain he is that the observed differences are real differences, or how much confidence he has that his conclusions are reliable. Estimating population values from samples, and qualifying these estimates by error statements based on probability theory, these are the two key elements of inferential statistics.

The typical design of a sample study can be illustrated like this:

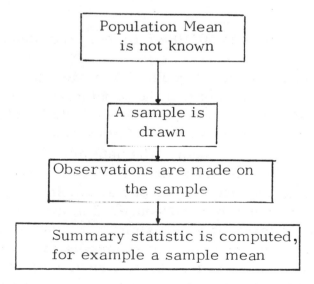

On the basis of such a design one can state what the sample mean is. However, that is usually not what the researcher wishes to know. Instead, he would like to determine the population mean.

There is no exact method to determine the population mean, of course, since in a sample study all one has is the mean of one sample. Can this information be used to estimate μ, the population mean? Yes, this can be done. Let us say we had recorded the number of times each book in a sample of ten has been checked out of the library for home use. The first book has gone six times since the library bought it. The second book went four times, and so on. Here are the data:

	Number of times checked out
Book 1	6
Book 2	4
Book 3	4
Book 4	8
Book 5	8
Book 6	7
Book 7	8
Book 8	6
Book 9	4
Book 10	5
	60

The mean for this sample comes to 60/10 = 6 times. The standard deviation is 1.7.

To estimate μ from this sample we could simply say that the sample mean is the best estimate we have and state that the population mean is probably about 6 times. But this statement lacks precision. It does not specify how far above or below the sample mean is "about". If more precision is desired, the normal curve can be used as a model. The data are simply converted to standard deviation form and the desired range of values is specified. This improves the crude first guess based on the one available sample mean.

Here is the reasoning behind this procedure. The mean of the ten sample observations is certainly different from, if similar to, the population mean. Seldom will a sample have the exact value as the population from which it came. If we drew another sample of ten observations, their mean also would approximate the true mean. We could draw many such samples and find that their means all differ more or less from the true mean. We would find that all our many sample means would form a distribution of their own, with a mean of means, $\overline{\overline{X}}$, and a standard deviation of means, $\sigma\overline{X}$. A moment's reflection shows that $\overline{\overline{X}}$, the mean of. all those sample means, would come very close to the population mean. And likewise, the standard deviation of this distribution of sample means, $\sigma\overline{X}$, usually called the standard error of the mean, would approach σ, the standard deviation of the population.

Now, not every one of the many sample means we might obtain in repeated sampling will be very close to the population mean, although most means will not fall far from μ. We might visualize the population by this curve:

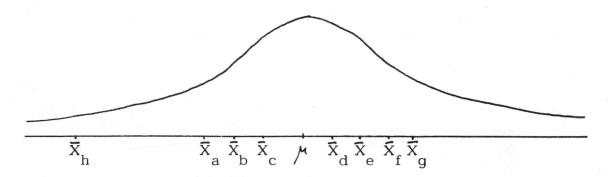

The points on the base line represent eight of the many possible hypothetical sample means obtained in repeated sampling. We see that $\overline{X}_a$ to $\overline{X}_g$ fall fairly close to μ, but that one mean, $\overline{X}_h$, departs considerably from the population value. For demonstration purposes, let us select three key values from this illustration, $\overline{X}_h$, $\overline{X}_c$, and μ.

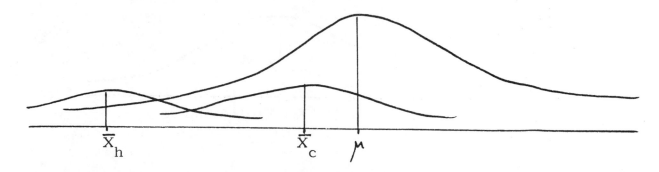

We can see that the curves representing the samples are flatter than the population curve. This is because there are fewer cases in the samples.

More importantly, we notice that μ and $\overline{X}_c$ are close together. The population mean falls approximately one standard deviation unit to the right of the sample mean. In fact, if we look at the previous illustration we will see that μ falls no farther away from any $\overline{X}$ than a few standard deviation units or fractions of units. With one exception: $\overline{X}_h$! This value is so far removed that μ falls far outside the z limits characteristic for the other seven sample means. We can use these theoretical considerations to develop a method of answering the question we are interested in: how close is our one sample mean to the population mean?

If the population mean were known to be $\mu = 8$, for example, just for demonstration's sake, and we had drawn a sample with a mean of $\overline{X} = 6$, we could draw a picture of our sample like this:

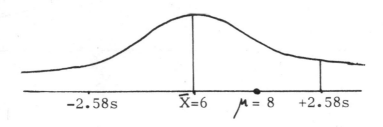

-2.58s $\overline{X} = 6$ $\mu = 8$ +2.58s

By luck we have drawn a sample that does indeed include μ within $\pm$ 2.58s. This factor of luck is, of course, unpredictable. What if we had drawn a different sample, say one with a mean of $\overline{X} = 10$?

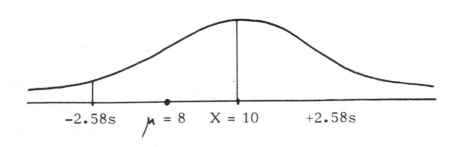

-2.58s $\mu = 8$ $X = 10$ +2.58s

Again we were lucky: the new sample also includes μ within +2.58s. In fact, we could draw one hundred different samples of ten and find that most sample means will include μ within those limits. Most, but probably not all! It is the nature of large numbers of chance events that, in the aggregate, they behave in predictable fashion. We could expect one maverick sample for every ninety-nine regular ones. Such a maverick might look like this:

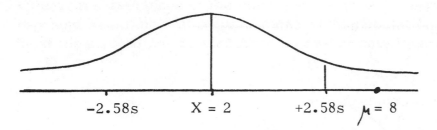

$$-2.58s \qquad X = 2 \qquad +2.58s \qquad \mu = 8$$

We note that this sample does not include μ within $\pm$ 2.58s of the sample mean.

The foregoing illustration shows that, in terms of our example problem, it would be reasonable to state that the population mean is contained within the interval bounded by a value 2.58 standard deviation units to the left and to the right of the sample mean, 6. What we are now looking for are two specific sample values, X_1 and X_2, that lie 2.58 standard deviation units to the left and to the right of 6. Such X values can be computed from the equation

$$z = \frac{X - \bar{X}}{\sigma}$$

The value of z is given as 2.58. The sample mean is known, $\bar{X} = 6$. What we do not have is the population standard deviation, σ. But we remember that the standard error of the mean approximates σ very closely. Unfortunately, the standard error of the mean, as we have described it, requires that we take a large number of samples, which in practice we cannot do. Instead, methods have been developed to estimate this standard error by using the one sample standard deviation, in this case, s = 1.7. The formula for the estimated standard error of the mean is

$$s\bar{X} = \frac{s}{\sqrt{N-1}}$$

Substituting the known sample values we obtain

$$s\bar{X} = \frac{1.7}{\sqrt{9}} = .563$$

We are now in a position to complete the computations for the desired confidence interval. For σ we substitute $s_{\overline{X}}$, the estimated standard error. We are looking for two values, X_1 and X_2, that fall 2.58 standard deviation units to the left and to the right of the sample mean, 6. This interval is computed by substituting all known values in the z equation:

$$z = \frac{X - \overline{X}}{\sigma} \longrightarrow \pm 2.58 = \frac{X - 6}{.563}$$

Solving for X_1 this becomes

$$X_1 = 6 + (-2.58)(.563) = 4.6$$

The other limit is obtained in analogous fashion:

$$X_2 = 6 + (2.58)(.563) = 7.4$$

By this detour over the model of the normal curve we have reached a point where we can say that there is confidence at the 99 per cent level (this is the meaning of "2.58", of course) that the interval from about 4.6 to about 7.4 contains the population mean. By specifying 99 per cent as the level of confidence we admit that one time in a hundred we will be wrong. One sample in a hundred will not contain μ within these limits, and we may have pulled this maverick sample! But, while we still do not and cannot know the exact value of μ, we have improved our first estimate ("the population mean is about 6") to a definite range of values, 4.6 to 7.4. This approach is all the more trustworthy because it includes a probability estimate of the error involved.

Often a researcher does not need such high confidence. Suppose we had been willing to settle for 5 chances in 100 of being wrong? We should have selected the 95 per cent level of confidence. The computations are as follows:

$$X_1 = 6 + (-1.96)(.563) = 4.91$$

and

$$X_2 = 6 + (1.96)(.563) = 7.1$$

Here is a picture of both confidence intervals superimposed:

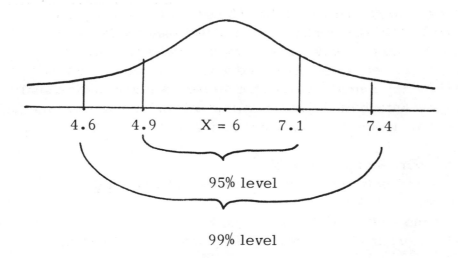

The illustration shows that if we select the 95 per cent level of confidence we come a little closer in our estimate. We say that the population mean is within narrower limits. But we pay for this closer estimate by greatly decreased confidence. We are now taking a risk of 1 in 20, not 1 in 100, that our sample is a maverick, one of those that do not contain μ within the specified limits.

Computing the confidence interval for a statistic is a standard procedure in sampling studies. In our examples we computed the 95 and the 99 per cent intervals for a mean by the formula

$$X \overset{+}{-} zs\overline{X}$$

where z was the standard score or normal deviate, X stood for the sample mean, and $s\overline{X}$ for the estimated standard error of the mean. But in library work we are often interested in other statistics than the mean -- percentages, proportions, correlation coefficients, to name a few. To the extent that we can estimate standard errors for such statistics we can compute confidence intervals. The general formula can be given as follows:

$$A \overset{+}{-} zsA$$

where A is any statistic derived from a sample, sA is the standard error of that statistic, and z is the normal deviate required for the desired confidence interval (found in a table such as Table C in Appendix 5).

Here is an example from a published article in <u>College and Research Libraries</u>. The investigator reported that 40 per cent in a sample of 250 junior college libraries use audiovisual techniques for library instruction. Had the author been interested in the status of library instruction in junior colleges nationwide he would have attempted an inference like this: "my sample shows that 40 per cent use audiovisual methods. What percentage of all junior college libraries use such methods?" Here are the steps that would have led to the answer:

1. The sample percentage is P = 40
2. The sample percentage of those not using audiovisual methods is Q = 100–P = 60
3. The size of the sample is N = 250
4. The standard error of a percentage is given by this formula

$$sP = \sqrt{\frac{P \times Q}{N}} = \sqrt{\frac{40 \times 60}{250}} = 3.09$$

5. The z score for the 95 per cent level of confidence is 1.96
6. The 95 per cent confidence interval is

$$P \pm zsP$$

or $\quad 40 \pm (1.96)(3.09)$

or $\quad 40 \pm (appr.)$ 6 per cent

or $\quad$ 34 to 46 per cent

The answer then would have been that from 34 to 46 per cent of all junior college libraries employ audiovisual methods for instruction.

The formula for the confidence interval sometimes contains the standard error in a different dress. In a communication published in the <u>Journal of the American Society for Information Science</u> there is a report concerning the characteristics of index entries in a certain abstract journal. The authors state that the standard error, σ_n, of the sampling distribution can be calculated by the expression

$$\sigma_n = \left[C(1-C)/N \right]^{1/2}$$

where C represents the proportion of irretrievable units in a random sample of N units.

Since $\left(\dfrac{x}{y}\right)^{\frac{1}{n}}$ is equivalent to $\sqrt[n]{\dfrac{x}{y}}$, we recognize that this

expression is identical to the one introduced for the previous example:

$$sP = \sqrt{\frac{P \times Q}{N}}$$

In the index entry article, one of the many percentages observed came to 52. The authors report as follows:

"Russian papers (approximately 12% of the sample) contained 52 % (σ_n = 4.0) title irretrievable

concepts compared with..."

Reporting percentages observed as well as the associated standard errors is good practice because it enables the serious reader to form a clear concept of the precision of the results. The skilled librarian instantly realizes what the probable range of the population values is, since he knows that at the 95 per cent level of confidence such a range is equal to the observed sample value plus or minus two times (1.96 times, to be exact) the standard error.

In another place in the same report the authors end a paragraph with this statement:

"Excluding terms in the miscellaneous category, R would range from 31% to 48% for a two parameter search"

Notice how carefully this conclusion is worded. By reporting even simple fact finding research in terms of estimated ranges, the authors succeed in gaining the confidence of their readers much more readily than if they had off-handedly claimed R to be "about 50 per cent", or had simply reported a sample value of 40 per cent.

12. SAMPLING

Suppose an investigator wanted to know how long, on the average, patrons in public libraries keep the materials they borrow from the record collection. The first question in this as in all research projects is to define the population about which one needs to have information.

Ideally, the researcher may be interested in the totality of all phonodisc loan transactions completed in all American (or perhaps Western or New York) public libraries, past, present, and future. Of course there is simply no way to achieve this goal because this is an infinite population -- time has not ended yet. What is done instead, of course, is to take a sample of borrowers, determine the average holding time of borrowed phonodiscs in the sample, and make inferences from these sample results to the population of all borrowers.

Sampling is a distinct branch of statistics, almost a field of study in its own right about which volumes have been written. We can mention here only the key principles. There are many methods of sampling. The simplest kind of sample is the convenience sample. The investigator picks the first 15 or 20 people that walk into the record room and calls this group his sample. Such a sample yields good data but when it comes to extending the sample findings to the whole population the investigator is left with the nagging suspicion that, since the sample consisted of the first few people who arrived in the morning, they were all early risers and were perhaps not truly representative of the entire population of potential borrowers. We say that such convenience samples are biased.

To put a research effort on a rigorous footing one must see to it that one's decisions are based on unbiased samples. When an investigator attempts to draw population-wide inferences from samples he wants to be sure that those samples are truly representative of the population studied. There is at least one recorded instance in the annals of survey research of a major error caused by neglect of this principle. When the editors of the Literary Digest conducted their by now famous poll in 1936 they drew a sample of American voters from the telephone directory and predicted a landslide victory for Alfred M. Landon. After Franklin D. Roosevelt had won the election it became obvious that the cause of the error had been a non-representative sample.

Today, the standard method of achieving an unbiased sample is the random or probability sample. In a properly planned random sample the items are drawn completely at random from the entire population or universe. Each item, therefore, has an equal chance of being included in the sample and any possible systematic error or bias is eliminated. The ideal way to select a random sample is to drop the entire population into a box, shake it, and pull one item out. Then replace it, shake the box once more, and pull another item. And so on until a sufficient sample has been drawn. Often one cannot manipulate a population in this way. But one can list the members, number them consecutively, and use a table of random numbers to simulate the box action with pencil and paper.

This is very easy to do. There are many published tables of random numbers, one of the best known being the Rand Corporation's One million random digits. Many textbooks in statistics include small but useful tables of random numbers in the appendix. Here is a fictitious excerpt from a table of random numbers:

10480	10750
22368	97458
24130	35249
42167	38980
37570	92140
74976	68763
35553	17960
35638	71944
74815	54684
45246	25282

To use such a table one simple points the pencil to any one number. If a three digit number between 001 and 999 is required, for example, one then decides which three digits of the five digit random number to pick -- perhaps the first three. Next, one establishes a suitable interval -- perhaps the first number in each block of five. One then selects as many numbers as are needed to make the sample. If a number is pulled twice one skips it and proceeds to the next. No number must appear more than once. In the example, let us say, the following numbers were selected from the first in each block of five:

104, 107, 687, and 749

These numbers are matched with the corresponding numbered population members that now constitute a random sample of four.

If a computer is available it is even easier. All one needs to do is call for the random number generator program available on most installations. The machine then prints out any desired list of random digits.

Frequently in the library field it is not possible to assign numbers to the members of a population. A sampling study involving all the cards in a library's shelf list, for example, cannot make use of the random number table method of sample selection because it would be much too costly to assign consecutive numbers to all shelf list cards. In such situations one often takes recourse to a systematic instead of a random sample. For systematic sampling one needs to know two things: the total number of units in the population, say 100,000 cards, and the size of the desired sample, say 1,000 cards. The quotient of these two numbers, 100,000/1,000, yields the sampling interval, 100. This means that every one hundredth card is pulled to make up a sample that approximates randomness. Provided, that is, no cyclical or other systematic fluctuations or biases are inherent in the population. The moment systematic bias enters into the sampling design the entire research project may be jeopardized, as the following fictitious episode will show.

A random selection of newspaper editorials was to be taken from a microfilm collection of the New York Times, filling twenty drawers of a cabinet. Each year of the subscription filled exactly twelve reels of microfilm, and these were arranged in columns of six reels each, beginning with May of a certain year in the upper left hand drawer. It was decided to use systematic sampling. Every twelfth reel was picked. The investigator did not realize until it was too late that all the editorials in the resulting sample were written in the merry month of May, hardly a random sample and probably not representative of all past editorials.

On occasion we know beforehand that our population is composed of two or more smaller homogeneous groups or strata. The proper design under such circumstances calls for a stratified random sample where a proportionately sized random sample is taken from each of the groups that together constitute the population.

Sometimes sampling must proceed in stages. It may simply be too expensive to draw a simple random sample. In such cases it is often possible to select, not individual items, but whole clusters of items. Each cluster is then treated as a little population and a random sample is drawn from it. Other variations of random sampling have been devised. All of them tend to buy time or money at the expense of sampling error since every step away from pure random sampling necessarily increases the probability of bias appearing in the sample.

Once the researcher settles the question of what kind of sample to take he must face the next question: how large a sample should he have? Does it matter how large a sample one takes? Suppose an investigator wished to know the average number of halftone and color illustrations per book in a population consisting of two thousand books classified in Dewey class 500. If he selected only one book, and that book had no illustrations whatsoever, could he reasonably conclude from this sample of one that science books have no illustrations? Hardly. We would have very little faith in this conclusion. Would a sample of two books be better? Or at what point would we begin to have faith? Perhaps the study requires a sample of one hundred books. We would probably be quite ready to accept an average value computed from a sample of one hundred books as a pretty fair estimate of the population average. But we still have doubts. We fear that one hundred, after all, is quite a small sample from a population of two thousand. We would feel more confident with two hundred or four hundred books in the sample. Intuitively we sense that an estimate of a population value from a sample improves in accuracy as the sample size increases. And if we were concerned with this topic for conversation's sake only we might leave it at that. However, we must know more if we are to be able to develop meaningful research designs. We must know precisely what size sample to select for a given study. It must be large enough to inspire confidence in the results. But how large is large enough? The answer depends on two decisions, both arbitrary and entirely subjective in nature. The first decision can be seen as one of precision. How precise an estimate of the population value do we wish to achieve? In the example involving the two thousand science books, can we be satisfied with an estimate of plus or minus fifty illustrations or do we need to know the average to whithin five illustrations?

The second decision is a question of confidence. Granting that all samples fluctuate around the true or population value, i.e. contain some amount of sampling error, how large a probability of being wrong in our estimate can we accept? In practice, this question is usually asked in terms of certain standard confidence levels. We ask ourselves, do we have to be 99 per cent sure that our estimate is correct within the precision boundaries stated, or can we accept the probability of being wrong five times in a hundred, can we operate at the 95 per cent level of confidence?

Both decisions, as we have stated, are arbitrary. The investigator must use judgement and past experience. He should ask himself, what are the consequences of being wrong? If a life is at stake (it never is in library science, at least not directly) we may have to insist on a narrow precision with a chance of error no more than one in a thousand

(99.9 per cent confidence level). As we shall see in a moment, this may require a large sample. If only minor consequences ensue, such as in a preliminary survey, we may still wish for narrow precision but be willing to gamble on the basis of five chances in a hundred of being wrong (95 per cent confidence level). This may reduce the size of the sample required. Or we may wish to relax our precision standard a little but insist on the 99 per cent level of confidence. Whatever the decision, once it is made the rest of the job of sample size determination reduces to a set of simple calculations.

The reader should notice that the determination of sample size is a question of confidence interval. The general formula for a confidence interval was given as follows:

$$Y_e = A \pm zs_A$$

where Y_e was an estimated value, A was a sample statistic such as the mean, z was the confidence level, and s_A the standard error of the statistic A.

The question of precision may be seen as one of determining the amount to be added to and deducted from the sample statistic in order to fix the range of precision of the estimate. In the formula given above the term zs_A stands for this amount. The value of s_A, in this case the standard error of the mean, can be defined as

$$s_A = s_{\bar{X}} = \frac{s}{\sqrt{n}}$$

where $s_{\bar{X}}$ is the estimated standard error of the mean, s is the standard deviation of the sample, and n is the sample size. It is therefore possible to visualize the amount of sampling error, or precision, usually called E, as follows:

$$zs_A = E = (z)\left(\frac{s}{\sqrt{n}}\right)$$

Once we see the question of precision as a relationship between confidence level, sample standard deviation, and sample size, it is easy to determine one of these three unknowns the moment two of them are fixed. And we already saw that two of them were indeed fixed, if only by arbitrary decisions.

Given a value of z and one of E, n can be computed from these equivalent relationships:

$$E = \frac{zs}{\sqrt{n}}$$

$$E^2 = \frac{z^2 s^2}{n}$$

$$n = \frac{z^2 s^2}{E^2}$$

To bring the example to a conclusion, let us say we had settled for a precision of plus or minus five illustrations with confidence desired at the 99 per cent level. We now have these values:

$$z = 2.58 \text{ (from the normal curve)}$$

$$E = 5 \quad \text{(an arbitrary decision)}$$

To complete the formula we need a value for s, the sample standard deviation. There is no way to know this value, of course, since we have not taken the sample yet. But by some bootstrap reasoning we can estimate the value. One method consists of taking a pilot sample of about fifty units, compute the standard deviation for it, and use this value instead of s. Suppose the researcher had done this and obtained a mean of 100 and a standard deviation of 25 illustrations. The required sample size can now be computed as follows:

$$n = \frac{(2.58)^2 \times (25)^2}{5^2} = \frac{(6.66) \times (625)}{25} = \frac{4162.5}{25} = 167$$

In the example, then, a sample of 167 units taken at random from the population would assure the investigator that the actual mean number of illustrations per book will not vary by more than five illustrations from the sample value 99 times in a hundred. If these specifications are acceptable, 167 is the ideal sample size for this project.

In many library research projects we do not achieve measurement on an interval scale. We may have data expressed only as a percentage of some total. For example, we may wish to know the error rate in a card catalog. Let us say we measured this error rate in terms of misfiled cards as a percentage of all cards filed. And let us say we had ten thousand filed cards in the catalog from which population we had taken a sample of one thousand cards. We found that one hundred of these had been misfiled. This corresponds to an error rate of ten per cent.

Suppose we wanted to know the population percentage to whithin plus or minus 2 per cent, at the 99 per cent confidence level. This means that we want to be sure 99 times in a hundred that the actual error rate in the catalog is somewhere between 8 and 12 per cent. The question is, was the sample of 1,000 books sufficiently large?

A formula for estimating the required sample size for a population whose elements fall into one of two possible categories (such as "filed correctly" or "filed incorrectly") is often given as

$$n = \frac{4\ pq}{L^2}$$

where n is the sample size, p is the proportion of elements in one of two categories, q is the proportion of elements in the other category, and L is the desired limit of error. This formula requires an advance estimate of p. Also, the product pq varies little between $p = .35$ and $p = .65$. Consequently, it must be used with great care when the proportions approach the value $p = q = .5$.

Furthermore, the formula does not take the size of the population into account. Snedecor and Cochran (Entry 57.a in the General Bibliography) suggest an additional step to correct for small population sizes:

$$n' = \frac{n}{1 + \phi}$$

where n' (enn prime) is the revised estimate of sample size, and ϕ (the Greek letter phi) is the quotient of n divided by the population size. Fortunately, shortcuts to sample size computations have been invented.

Arkin and Colton (Entry 2 in the General Bibliography) have provided a table for problems of this kind. Given the population size (here: 10,000), the confidence level (here: 99 per cent), and the reliability (what we have termed precision, here: ± 2 per cent), their table says that a sample of at least 2932 units is required. But we had a sample of only 1000 units. What does this mean in terms of our decision? The table tells us that, at the 99 per cent level, a sample of 1000 will guarantee us at best a precision of ± 4 per cent. In other words, we have no choice but to settle for a wider confidence interval. The best we can say is that the population value is probably between 6 and 14 per cent.

Now, if an error rate of 5 per cent is administratively all we can tolerate, the information gained from the sample is certainly useful. It tells us that we are almost certainly in trouble. The chance of our sample having come from a population with an error rate of less than 5 per cent is extremely small.

In many real life situations of this nature a confidence interval this large (± 4 per cent) is intolerable. The prospective investigator should therefore consider the risks and penalties of inadequate sample size before drawing the sample, since misjudgements of this nature are hard to correct later without increasing the cost of the research.

Arkin's table value of n, the required sample size, is based on the frequency distribution of P, the percentage of cases in the population. It is a model based on the hypergeometric probability which takes into account the size of the population from which the sample is to be drawn. Since the model works only for populations that are large in relation to the sample size, care must be taken by the investigator to avoid claiming unwarranted precision levels for samples drawn from small populations. Since few investigators in the library field or, for that matter, in most other fields of research, will be prepared to apply the sophisticated mathematical reasoning required to take all the details of sampling theory

into consideration when designing a plan of research it is perhaps
best for most of us to consult a statistician at the point where kind and
size of sample have to be determined.

There is one particularly treacherous false belief about sampling
that persists widely. It is that sample size is a percentage of the
population which increases linearly and directly as the population
increases. If 100 units is an adequate sample from a population of
1000 (10 per cent), many believe that consequently a population of
2000 units requires a sample of 200 (10 per cent) for comparable
results. The fallacy is based on the assumption that if a sample of
100 yields an error rate of E, then a sample of 200, everything else
being equal, should yield an improved error rate of E/2; or that
doubling the sample size doubles the precision. And this is false.

Consider a sample of size n = 100 with a standard deviation of
s = 25. Obviously, the estimated standard error of the mean
amounts to

$$s_{\overline{X}} = \frac{s}{\sqrt{n}} = \frac{25}{\sqrt{100}} = 2.5$$

Because the sampling error E varies directly with the size of the
standard error $(E = zs_{\overline{X}})$, we know that with a standard error twice
the size $(s_{\overline{X}} = 5)$ we would have achieved half the precision:

$$z(2s_{\overline{X}}) = 2E$$

Likewise, a standard error of 1.25 would have given us half the
sampling error or, which is the same thing, twice the precision

$$z(\frac{s_{\overline{X}}}{2}) = \frac{E}{2}$$

As the reader knows, the formula for the estimated standard error
of the mean has the square root of n in the denominator. This means
that doubling n will certainly affect the standard error, but it will
not double it. We can conduct a little demonstration to show what
happens when we double n. Let us double n four times in succession.
Here is the resulting distribution:

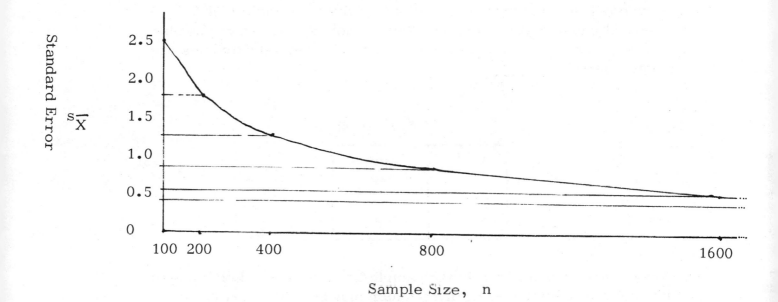

What the graph shows is that after a certain break-even point is reached doubling the sample size will double the investigator's work load without appreciably improving anything else. This is why the wise researcher discounts the myth of the fixed percentage sample and bases his decision instead on a sample of a size consistent with the desired precision and confidence level.

13.   HYPOTHESIS TESTING
         (ONE SAMPLE)

In the field of library science one kind of problem occurs frequently. It is the case where a researcher is interested in the difference between the proportions of cases from a sample that fall into several categories. A certain phenomenon may have two possible outcomes, A and B. A sample is taken and the observed outcomes are tabulated like this:

Observations

A	40
B	60

Obviously, each observation in the sample fits into one and only one of the two cells of the table. An investigator may be interested in the difference between these proportions, and the significance of that difference. One statistical test often recommended for this design is the chi square test (χ^2). The chi square statistic is based on the difference between an observed number of cases falling in each of several mutually exclusive categories and an expected number of such cases. The expectations are derived from a null hypothesis of presumed proportions in the population studied.

The chi square test has been described in many books but most prominently by Siegel (Entry 54 in the General Bibliography):

$$\chi^2 = \sum_{i=1}^{k} \frac{(O_i - E_i)^2}{E_i}$$

This formula is often shortened to read $\chi^2 = \sum \frac{(O - E)^2}{E}$ where O

(the letter O) refers to the actual observations in a category and E stands for the expected number of observations. Thus for a two cell design the expectation usually is that 50 out of a hundred observations should fall in each category (E = ½N). A complete two-cell chi square design might look like this:

	O	E
A	40	50
B	60	50

As the table shows, the actual observations, one hundred in number, differ from the way they were expected to distribute themselves in the two categories A and B. The chi square statistic for this difference can be computed as follows:

$$\chi^2 = \sum \frac{(O-E)^2}{E}$$

$$= \frac{(40-50)^2}{50} + \frac{(60-50)^2}{50}$$

$$= \frac{100}{50} + \frac{100}{50}$$

$$= 4$$

Chi square tables such as Table E in Appendix 5 have been computed to enable the researcher to determine whether such a computed value is statistically significant. In this case, the required chi square value for significance at the 99 per cent confidence level is 6.63 or better. The obtained value is only 4. The researcher would have to accept the null hypothesis of no difference. This means that the observed difference between the categories (60-40=20) can be considered to be a chance occurrence, or that the research produced no evidnece that there was a real difference in the population from which the sample came.

A warning must be sounded here, however. The chi square test is based on the number of categories established, or more technically, on the degrees of freedom that obtain in the model. Unfortunately, chi square is also sensitive to the number of observations. If there are fewer than five expectations in one of the cells of a two-cell design (d.f.=1) the test has been found invalid. To overcome this handicap of the small cell frequencies Siegel and others have suggested combining two or more categories to increase the number of observations per cell. For it has been found that increased cell frequencies lead to higher values of chi square. In fact, under the 50-50 hypothesis (E = ½N) the value of chi square increases in direct proportion to the number of observations. This means that a large (significant) chi square value can be the result of either one of two unrelated factors: a large difference or a large number of observations.

Consider the following two-cell chi square design where N is equal to 1,000:

	O	E
A	400	500
B	600	500

Although the difference between the number of observations in cell A and those in cell B is proportionally equal to that of the design of page 139 the chi square for this table comes to $\chi^2 = 40$. Since the number of degrees of freedom has not changed, this value is interpreted as highly significant, which, of course, is absurd.

This is why Siegel recommended the use of the z test when N is large. He proposed the followign formula:

$$z = \frac{(x + .5) - NP}{\sqrt{NPQ}}$$

where x is the smaller of the observed frequencies. When E equals ½N this is equivalent to

$$z = \frac{(x + .5) - N/2}{\sqrt{N/4}}$$

But this formula, too, yields higher z values for large samples than for small samples and is, therefore, no improvement over the chi square test.   Here is the z test for the data of page 139:

	Observed	Proportion expected
A	40	.5
B	60	.5

$$z = \frac{(x + .5) - N/2}{\sqrt{N/4}} = \frac{(40 + .5) - 50}{\sqrt{25}} = -1.9 \text{ (not significant)}.$$

And here is the z test for the data of page 140:

	Observed	Proportion expected
A	400	.5
B	600	.5

$$z = \frac{(x + .5) - N/2}{\sqrt{N/4}} = \frac{(400 + .5) - 500}{\sqrt{250}} = -6.29 \text{ (highly significant)}.$$

Although the proportions have not changed in the second example we have achieved a significant difference by the expedient of picking a larger sample. Clearly, neither chi square nor the z test can be recommended for studies of differences in categories when large samples are involved.

14. HYPOTHESIS TESTING
(TWO SAMPLES)

Another very common problem in library research involves the evaluation of the difference between two sample means. Let us say a library had been conducting a certain operation L. The effect of this operation can be measured by a criterion C. When several units are observed (a sample), a criterion score is obtained for each member and a mean for the sample can be computed as $\overline{C}_L$.

Now a modification K is introduced. Another sample is taken and the criterion scores for it are summed and divided by N yielding a second mean, $\overline{C}_K$. Graphically we can represent the procedure as follows:

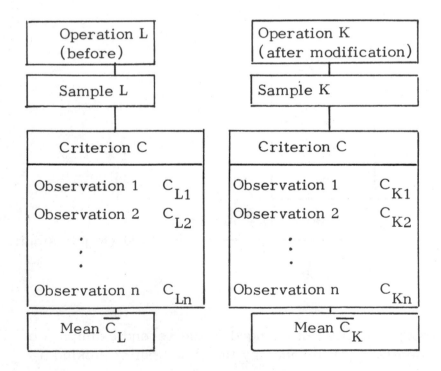

If the two means $\overline{C}_L$ and $\overline{C}_K$ are exactly alike, i.e. if the difference
D between them is zero, we can say with confidence that modification
K has no effect on the criterion measure C. We can say that our two
samples came from the same population or from two populations that
are identical in respect to the criterion.

If D were not zero but very small, we might say that our two samples
could have come from two different populations, that the modification
K had an effect on the criterion score. But we could also reason that
the difference observed was merely a chance variation, that the modification really had no effect at all.

If D were very large, on the other hand, we would say that our two
samples definitely came from different populations, that the modification
did have a differential effect on the criterion scores. The trick is to know
at what point to decide that the observed difference D is larger than
could be explained by chance.

In the example experiment just presented we presumed that modification
K would affect criterion measure C. We hypothesized that the mean
score "before" would be different from the mean score "after", or
in symbols:

$$H_1: \quad \overline{C}_L \neq \overline{C}_K$$

where H_1 stands for "research hypothesis" and $\neq$ means "not equal".
But this hypothesis is hard if not impossible to test. For whenever the
difference between two values is as great as even .0001 units -- a very
small difference -- the two values are obviously not equal any longer.
Yet we would certainly not use this infinitesimal inequality to settle the
question whether modification K has a differential effect on the scores.

To get at the question how large a difference it is that makes two such
means unequal enough for a decision we resort to a stratagem. We
formulate a null hypothesis, a hypothesis of no difference, as follows:

$$H_0: \quad \overline{C}_L = \overline{C}_K$$

To test this null hypothesis we theorize as follows. Any sample is
a chance event. We could have picked a maverick sample K, one that
happens to show a huge difference when there really is no difference
in the population. Likewise, we could have picked a sample K that
shows practically no difference when in reality there is a sizeable
difference.

To visualize the possible kinds of samples we could have picked, we present here a well known four cell table of sampling errors:

	The null hypothesis is TRUE (there really is a difference)	The null hypothesis is FALSE (there really is not a difference)
We reject the null hypothesis	Type I error	Correct decision
We accept the null hypothesis	Correct decision	Type II error

In our imaginary experiment we were primarily interested in guarding against a Type I error. We do not want to reject the null hypothesis when in reality it is true. We do not want to jump to the conclusion that the modification was effective when in reality it was not.

Needless to say, we do not want to commit a Type II error either. Suppose the modification was really effective. We certainly do not want to deny this by accepting the null hypothesis falsely. Whether to run the risk of a Type I or a Type II error is a question of utility since the probability of one increases as the other decreases. When the consequences of mistaking a chance difference for a genuine difference are too costly and the risk of such an error must be minimized, a conservative level of significance is set, avoiding the Type I error. When, on the other hand, there is a search for all promising leads and no genuine prospect can be overlooked, a liberal level of significance is elected, avoiding a Type II error.

Once these alternatives and their consequences have been weighed, a researcher is likely to conclude a data analysis with a statement of this kind: "the probability of a difference D as large or larger than the one observed having arisen by chance is α ", where α is a small probability such as .05 or .01.

This conclusion is reached by reference to a model such as the normal curve. For if we drew many pairs of samples, each pair would yield a difference. We could plot these differences as if they were data in their own right. Under the null hypothesis of no difference, the mean of this distribution of differences would be zero ($\overline{D} = 0$). The many differences would be normally distributed around their mean of zero. Here is a picture of this distribution:

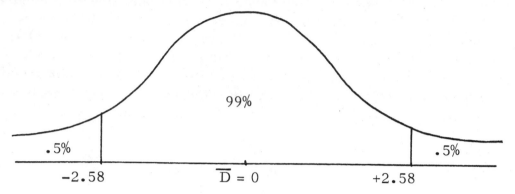

This, of course, is only a theoretical concept, a model. We must now convert our one real observed difference, D, into a z score so that we can stretch it over the model and make probability statements. Such a z score has this form:

$$z = \frac{D - \overline{D}}{\sigma}$$

where σ is the theoretical standard deviation of the model distribution of differences. But, of course, we do not know this value σ. Instead, we can estimate the standard error of the difference as an approximation and use this estimate in place of the σ in the formula. The estimated standard error of the difference has this form:

$$s_D = \sqrt{s\overline{C}_L{}^2 + s\overline{C}_K{}^2}$$

where $s\overline{C}_L{}^2$ and $s\overline{C}_K{}^2$ are the squared standard errors of the two sample distributions. This value in place of σ yields the following formula for the z score:

$$z = \frac{D - \overline{D}}{s_D}$$

Next, we select a confidence level, say α = .01, which means that we want to be 99 per cent certain that the difference observed is not a chance difference. We compare the computed z value with a table to find out how close to the critical ratio, the tabled value for α = .01, it is.

If the observed z is equal to or larger than the critical (tabled) value we reject the null hypothesis and say that a difference of this size would have happened by chance less than one time in a hundred.

Here is another fictitious example. In a study of different ways of orienting new students to a school library one group (Group I) was given a lecture and tour. Another group (Group II) got to see a slide-tape orientation program instead. A week after the beginning of school both groups were given a library search efficiency test. Here are the resulting scores:

	Group I	Group II
Sample size N:	101	101
Mean:	100	110
Standard deviation:	9	8

The hypothesis under consideration was that one of the methods of orientation would be more effective than the other in terms of search efficiency scores. The hypothesis was formulated as follows:

$$H_1: \quad Mean_I \neq Mean_{II}$$

For testing purposes this was converted to a null hypothesis:

$$H_0: \quad Mean_I = Mean_{II}$$

or a difference of zero. It was decided that a probability of committing a Type I error of .01 or less was acceptable ($\alpha = .01$). Here are the requisite computations. First we have these standard errors:

$$s\overline{X}_I = \frac{s_I}{\sqrt{n-1}} = \frac{9}{10} = .9$$

and

$$s\overline{X}_{II} = \frac{s_{II}}{\sqrt{n-1}} = \frac{8}{10} = .8$$

Their squares are .81 and .64, respectively. This gives us an estimated standard error of the difference:

$$s_D = \sqrt{.81 + .64} = \sqrt{1.45} = 1.2$$

Substituting this value in the formula for z we have:

$$z = \frac{D - \overline{D}}{s_D} = \frac{(100-110) - 0}{1.2} = -8.3$$

A look at the model shows us that the obtained z value of −8.3 is definitely in the rejection region:

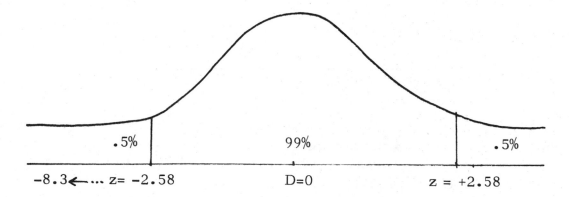

.5% 99% .5%

−8.3 ←··· z= −2.58   D=0   z = +2.58

We say that the probability of a z as large or larger than the one observed (-8.3) having arisen by chance from two equivalent populations is less than α = .01. We therefore reject the null hypothesis. We have reason to believe that the two populations were not equivalent, that the slide-tape orientation program caused the observed improvement in search efficiency scores in Group II.

Often we must deal with samples so small that the normal curve model is invalid. But we can apply a different model, the t distribution (often referred to as student's t, after "student", the pseudonym of William Sealy Gossett who first developed this method of estimating a population mean on the basis of a very small sample). The computation of the t value is identical to that for z. The smaller sample size, of course, results in different standard errors:

$$s\overline{X}_I = \frac{9}{\sqrt{10}} = \frac{9}{3.16} = 2.84$$

and

$$s\overline{X}_{II} = \frac{8}{\sqrt{10}} = \frac{8}{3.16} = 2.53$$

Using these estimated standard errors of the sample means we obtain the estimated standard error of the difference:

$$s_D = \sqrt{s\overline{X}_I^2 + s\overline{X}_{II}^2} = \sqrt{8.06 + 6.4} = 3.8$$

The t formula is the same as the one for z:

$$t = \frac{(X_I - X_{II}) - D}{s_D} = \frac{(100-110)-0}{3.8} = \frac{-10}{3.8} = -2.63$$

At the specified α level for 10 degrees of freedom the t model looks like this (see also Table D in Appendix 5):

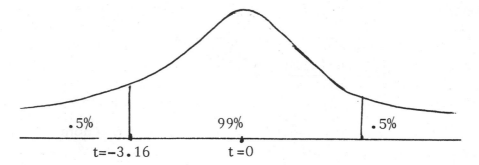

.5%   99%   .5%

t=-3.16   t =0

We can see that the observed value of t= -2.63 lies in the acceptance region. The null hypothesis must be accepted. For this fictitious project this means that there is no evidence that one of the two methods is superior to the other.

Many times in library research we do not have scores on an interval scale but data on a categorical or nominal scale. Such data are not isomorphic to the arithmetic number system and the difference between two groups, therefore, cannot be evaluated in terms of means. Methods have been developed, however, to evaluate the significance of the difference between two proportions. Here is an example. One hundred newly graduated librarians and one hundred experienced librarians were asked, among other things, what they thought of a certain set of reference books. Of the one hundred newly graduated librarians, the proportion that liked the set was .68. Of the one hundred experienced librarians, the proportion was .88. The question to be answered next was if there was a significant difference between the two classes of librarians in terms of their opinions. The confidence level was set at α = .01.

This problem can be solved by a t test for the difference between two proportions. The formula for samples of equal size is:

$$t = \frac{p_1 - p_2}{\sqrt{\dfrac{2 p_e q_e}{N}}}$$

where p_e is the simple mean of p_1 and p_2, and q_e equals $1.0 - p_e$.

Substituting the known values in the formula we have:

$$t = \frac{.68 - .88}{\sqrt{\dfrac{2(.78)(.22)}{100}}} = \frac{-.2}{\sqrt{.0034}} = -3.42$$

Table D in Appendix 5 shows that for 100 degrees of freedom a t value of $\pm$ 2.62 or greater is required to reject the null hypothesis at the specified level of α = .01. As the model shows, a t of –3.42 is in the rejection region.

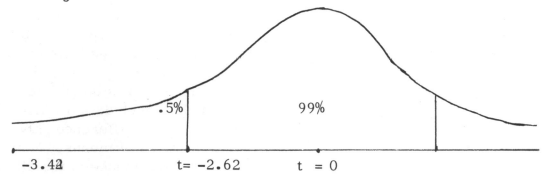

The researcher would reject the null hypothesis and state with 99 per cent confidence that the new librarians differ decidedly from the experienced librarians in terms of their opinions concerning the set.

When the samples are of unequal size ($N_1 \neq N_2$) a slightly different formula applies:

$$t = \frac{P_1 - P_2}{\sqrt{p_e q_e \left(\dfrac{N_1 + N_2}{N_1 N_2}\right)}}$$

where p_e is the weighted mean of the proportions:

$$p_e = \frac{N_1 P_1 + N_2 P_2}{N_1 + N_2}$$

Here is a practical example based on an actual report published in a library science periodical. In a small college library students kept taking books home without charging them at the desk. An experiment was tried to see if an honor system (do-it-yourself charging) would reduce this wildcat borrowing.

Before the honor system was put into effect, a sample of 254 students were asked if they do take books home without charging. A total of 103 students admitted they did. After the honor system was put into effect another sample of 546 students were asked the same question. A total of 176 said they did take books home uncharged.

The research design measured the difference between the two groups in terms of the proportion of yes answers, p, in relation to N, the number of students in each of the samples. The hypothesis tested was that there is no difference in terms of p between the two groups, with a confidence level of α = .01. Here are the data. The proportion in the first sample, p_1, was .4. The proportion in the second sample, p_2, was .32. The difference between these two proportions was .4 – .32 $\doteq$ .08. The t value was computed as follows:

$$t = \frac{.08}{\sqrt{(.34)(.66)\left(\frac{800}{138,684}\right)}} = \frac{.08}{.036} = 2.22$$

The tabled value for t at the .01 level for this size sample is 2.58. Since the t computed from the data is clearly less there is no reason to reject the null hypothesis. As far as the experiment goes the conclusion must be that the honor system has no effect on wildcat borrowing.

In the preceding example the researcher could not be sure whether the honor system might reduce or increase wildcat borrowing, if it brought about any change at all. This is why he tested the data against a two-tailed model. He expected the t value to be either positive or negative. Many times we know that the outcome is in a certain direction. This enables us to conduct a one tail test. This means that we compare the calculated t value to a model that has the expected probability all in one tail:

99%   1%

t = 2.32

Obviously, the critical value is lower for the one tail test, which in some cases enables a researcher to reject a null hypothesis that he would have to accept in a two tail test. This is a question of power, the sensitivity of the test employed to existing real differences. The test that has the highest probability of rejecting the null hypothesis when it is false has the highest power. A measure of power is often given as $1 - \beta$, where β is the probability of committing a Type II error. The question of β and the power functions for various kinds of statistical tests is a topic of mathematical statistics treated in many of the more comprehensive treatises mentioned in the General Bibliography. As a guideline it can be said that, everything else being equal, a one tail test is more powerful than a two tail test.

15. HYPOTHESIS TESTING
(TWO OR MORE SAMPLES)

When data are of interval or ratio quality, i.e. are capable of being summarized by a mean and a standard deviation, and we are interested in the differences between two or more samples subjected experimentally to different conditions analysis of variance is a possible method of data analysis. Suppose there were three different acoustic conditions in the reading rooms of a library: silence, soft music, and free conversation, and a researcher wished to determine if reading room acoustics have any effect on an active reader's level of attention to meaning and reading speed. He might suspect, for example, that the silent room results in better performance than the noisy room, all else being equal.

To find out he sets up an experiment. He finds some willing readers to serve as test subjects and assigns them at random to the three rooms that have been prepared and gives them identical reading tasks. Group I are those readers that are sent to the quiet room. Group II are sent to the music room. Group III are required to do their reading in the noisy room. At the end of the experiment all readers take the same evaluative test.

Let us say, for simplicity's sake, that the test scores were one digit numbers of interval quality. And let us further assume that there had been three readers in each group. The data, schematically, would look like this:

Group I		Group II		Group III	
Ss1	X_{I1}	Ss1	X_{II1}	Ss1	X_{III1}
Ss2	X_{I2}	Ss2	X_{II2}	Ss2	X_{III2}
Ss3	X_{I3}	Ss3	X_{II3}	Ss3	X_{III3}
$\sum X_I$		$\sum X_{II}$		$\sum X_{III}$	
Mean: $\overline{X}_I$		Mean: $\overline{X}_{II}$		Mean: $\overline{X}_{III}$	

We can expect that the nine individual scores in the experiment will differ from each other. The question is, do they differ because of individual differences and other chance factors operating among readers, or because of the influence of the different conditions, or both? Analysis of variance is a procedure for dividing the total variance of a series of observations into component parts, each of which is associated with a possible source of variation.

Let us put some very simple numbers into this imaginary experiment, just for demonstration purposes. Suppose the researcher had carefully matched the nine readers in terms of their reading ability and other important characteristics. He might obtain a set of data like these:

	Group I	Group II	Group III	
	2	3	4	
	2	3	4	
	2	3	4	
Sums:	6	9	12	27
Means:	2	3	4	3

We find that the three samples differ from each other only in their group means. There is no variability within groups. Since the investigator had taken care to match the readers selected as subjects in terms of their abilities he should interpret the findings as follows: the logically most plausible source of variation between the scores in this set of data is the difference between reading room conditions.

If, on the contrary, he had obtained data like these:

	Group I	Group II	Group III	
	2	1	0	
	3	3	3	
	4	5	6	
Sums:	9	9	9	27
Means:	3	3	3	3

he would conclude that reading room conditions apparently had no effect upon reading scores since the means of all three groups are identical.

All observed differences are accounted for by individual differences and chance effects operating within each group. No difference between groups is discernible.

Real life samples, or course, never yield such clear answers. There will be some variability within groups, and some between groups. When the variation within groups equals or exceeds the variability between groups we discount the effect of the conditions. If the situation is reversed, if there is more variability between groups than within groups, we tend to believe that there is a differential effect exercised by the conditions.

Variability is measured by the summary statistic s^2, the variance. In analysis of variance studies, variance computed on the basis of the difference between groups is called the "between-groups mean square", or MS_b. Variance within sample groups is called "within-groups mean square", MS_w. The quotient of these two variances,

$$\frac{MS_b}{MS_w}$$

is called the F ratio. This statistic serves as the ultimate criterion for inferences concerning the existence of a true difference between two or more experimental conditions.

If we could assign all readers in the world in turn to each of the three reading room conditions, somehow erasing their memories between tests, we should in each case obtain the universe of all possible reading test scores. Under the hypothesis that conditions made a difference, we would expect these three populations to have different mean reading scores. This is the significance of our research hypothesis:

$$H_1: \mu_I \neq \mu_{II} \neq \mu_{III}$$

To put this hypothesis to the test, however, requires a stratagem, for it is one of the peculiarities of the inductive method that no matter how many times we conduct this experiment and observe a difference, we will never be certain that all possible replications would yield a difference. One cannot prove universal statements such as "acoustical conditions affect reading scores". But one can easily disprove them. If we turn our hypothesis around and formulate the so-called null hypothesis,

$$H_0: \mu_I = \mu_{II} = \mu_{III}$$

we can see that it takes only one single observed difference to
disprove the statement that acoustical conditions do not influence
reading scores!

In reality, of course, investigators must be content with samples
since there is no way to capture the universe for experiments. In
the imaginary reading room study we employed three samples, three
groups of readers. We assumed that our samples were representative of
their populations. Therefore, in accord with the null hypothesis one
should assume that the group means will be equal, $\overline{X}_I = \overline{X}_{II} = \overline{X}_{III}$.
But of course, as samples go, even under the null hypothesis, that is,
even if the null hypothesis were true, they will not have exactly equal
means. The group means will differ more or less. If the same experiment were repeated many times with different samples one would
find that most of these differences would be very slight. A few samples
would show large differences.

We can take this reasoning a step further. Each set of three samples
yields an F ratio. The theoretical sampling distribution of F ratios is
known. If the null hypothesis were true and conditions really did not
affect the scores, the great majority of all theoretically possible sets
of three samples would yield F ratios at or near unity. This is so
because the differences within samples and the differences between
samples would tend to balance each other out. But there would be some
sample sets of three that show greater differences. There would be a
few sets that exhibit extreme variation one way, and none or very little
the other way.

But in experimental work we restrict ourselves to one single set of
samples. Suppose our single set of samples showed large "between"
variation and small "within" variation. In other words, we obtained
a high F ratio. We must then decide how to interpret the results. Since
we know that even under the null hypothesis there could be an extreme
sample, yielding a high F ratio, we could be cautious and decide that by
chance we happened to have pulled an unusual set of data, that there
really is no difference between conditions. On the other hand, since there
would be only a very few of these unusual sets under the null hypothesis,
the probability that our one set of three samples is one of them is
correspondingly low. To settle the question, we take our obtained F
ratio to the model of the theoretical F distribution. The model of the
F distribution has been tabulated in many books. Arkin, Entry 2 in the
General Bibliography, has included a convenient F table. We read out
of this table the probability that an F ratio of the magnitude yielded by our

data could have arisen by chance under the null hypothesis. This is the essence of analysis of variance.

In computing an F ratio from data one begins by treating all observations as if they were one big sample, i.e. disregarding groups. If we add all scores and divide by the total number of scores we obtain a combined mean for all observations. This is called the grand mean,

$$\overline{\overline{X}}$$

In accord with the null hypothesis ($H_0 : \overline{X}_I = \overline{X}_{II} = \overline{X}_{III}$) the grand mean is an estimate of the population mean, μ.

Now each of the observed scores varies more or less from this grand mean. We can tabulate these score deviations from the grand mean, square them, and sum the squares. And we can add up the resulting sums of squares to obtain the "total sum of squares", or SS_t.

Schematically, the genealogy of this sum of the group sums of the squared score deviations from the grand mean can be shown as follows:

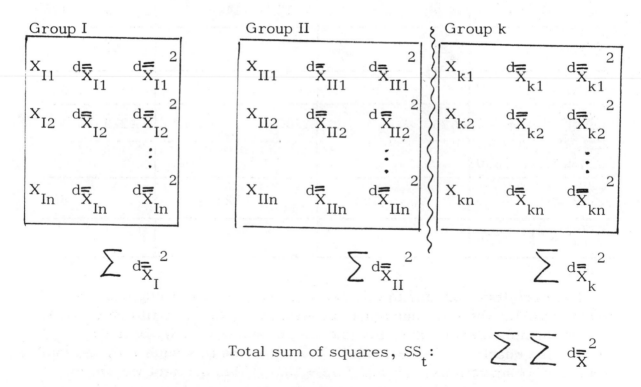

Total sum of squares, SS_t: $\sum \sum d_{\overline{\overline{X}}}^2$

In practical applications it is often not desirable to compute deviation scores and their squares. This equivalent computational formula is more convenient:

$$SS_t = \sum\left(\sum x^2\right) - \frac{\left(\sum\left(\sum x\right)\right)^2}{N}$$

where X stands for a raw score, and N is the total number of observations. We shall introduce another set of fictitious interval quality data to demonstrate the procedure of computing SS_t by means of the computational formula for raw scores:

	Group I		Group II		Group III	
	X	x^2	X	x^2	X	x^2
	5	25	10	100	11	121
	7	49	8	64	15	225
	2	4	7	49	15	225
	2	4	13	169	10	100
	9	81	12	144	14	196
$\sum x$	25		50		65	
$\sum\left(\sum x\right)$ 140						
$\left(\sum x\right)^2$	625		2500		4225	
$\sum\left(\sum x\right)^2$ 7350						
$\sum x^2$		163		526		867
$\sum\left(\sum x^2\right)$ 1556						

There are three groups in this set of data, and each group has five scores (n=5). The total number of observations, thus, is fifteen (N=15).

The formula directs us to find the sum of sums, $\sum\left(\sum x\right)$, or 140; to square that quantity, $140^2 = 19,600$; and to divide this square by the total number of observations: 19,600 / 15 = 1307. This quotient we are to deduct from the sum of the sums of the squared raw scores, 1,556. We now have

$$SS_t = 1,556 - 1,307 = 249$$

This total sum of squares represents the total variability in our set of three samples. It remains for us to isolate the two components of that total variability: the part caused by individual and chance differences within groups, and the part caused by the effect of the conditions between groups.

If the total sum of squares is based on score deviations from the grand mean it is easy to see that the within sum of squares must be based on score deviations fro the group means. This sum of the sums of the squared score deviations from their group means, SS_w for short, can be represented schematically as follows:

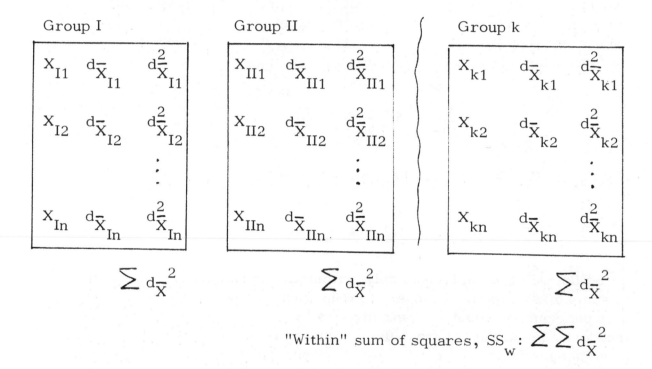

"Within" sum of squares, SS_w: $\sum\sum d_{\overline{X}}^2$

Again, there is a computational formula that works for sets of equal n:

$$SS_w = \sum(\sum x^2) - \frac{\sum(\sum x)^2}{n}$$

Continuing with the example of page 158 this formula directs us to find the sum of the squared group sums, 7,350; divide that quantity by n, 7,350 / 5 = 1,470; and subtract this quotient from the sum of sums of

160

the squared raw scores, 1,556. We now have

$$SS_w = 1,556 - 1,470 = 86$$

This within sum of squares is associated entirely with that part of the total variation that is due to chance factors and individual differences among subjects in a group. Possible differential effects of various experimental conditions do not effect this measure. It follows that if we subtract the within sum of squares from the total sum of squares we are left with the between sum of squares, or SS_b, a quantity that measures the effect of the experimental conditions:

$$SS_b = SS_t - SS_w$$

If we apply this formula to our fictitious set of data we obtain

$$SS_b = 249 - 86 = 163$$

So far we have performed only arithmetic operations that resulted in sums of squared deviations. To transform sums of squares to variances or mean squares requires their division by the appropriate degrees of freedom. Since the between sum of squares is based on the deviation of group means from the grand mean, the appropriate degrees of freedom are k-1. We must divide SS_b by k-1 to obtain the variance estimate due to group effects:

$$MS_b = \frac{SS_b}{k - 1}$$

The within sum of squares, on the other hand, is based on the deviation of individual scores from their group means. The proper degrees of freedom are $\Sigma (n-1)$ or N-k. The variance estimate due to chance effects is:

$$MS_w = \frac{SS_w}{N - k}$$

Our fictitious experimental data yield a between mean square of 163 / 2 = 81.5. They yield a within mean square of 86 / 12 = 7.1. A moment's reflection will show us that MS_b, being based on group means, is not a pure measure of the effect of the different experimental conditions applied to the groups but is contaminated by chance variations and individual differences among subjects. To filter out that chance variation and obtain a pure measure of the effect of the experimental conditions we must determine by how much the between groups variance exceeds the within groups variance. This is done by dividing the MS_b by the MS_w which gives us the desired F ratio:

$$F = \frac{81.5}{7.1} = 11.48$$

Since the tabled model value of F for 2 and 12 degrees of freedom, respectively, is 3.88 at the .01 level we can report that our obtained F has a probability of occurrence under the null hypothesis of

$$p < .01$$

This means that an F ratio of the magnitude reported would occur by chance alone less than once in a hundred equivalent experiments. We would reject the null hypothesis at the 99 per cent level and conclude that there is little likelyhood that the groups were equal. We would say that the experimental conditions did indeed influence the reading scores.

The results of an analysis of variance are often displayed in a summary table. For the imaginary problem just demonstrated we might draw up the following summary table:

Source of variation	SS	df	MS	F	Significance
Between groups	163	2	81.5	11.48	$p < .01$
Within groups	86	12	7.1		
Total	249	14			

From a summary table like this the reader can see at a glance how the total variance was partitioned into two sources, one part due to group differences ("between"), the other due to chance events ("within").

The analysis just described is the simplest in the family of analysis of variance techniques. It is suitable for problems where several samples are subjected to different states of one experimental condition and the decision has to be made whether these samples can be regarded as having come from different populations. This technique is usually referred to as one way analysis of variance. But many research problems are more complex. In a study of reading room conditions, for example, it is conceivable that the subject matter or difficulty of the reading matter may have an appreciable effect in addition to the room conditions. If we perform a one way analysis, the resulting F ratio tells us only that there is a difference between groups, not what the probable cause of that difference is. In this case, a one way analysis would not distinguish between the effects of room conditions and the effects of reading matter. It is possible, for example, that the entire observed difference is due to room conditions, reading matter making no difference whatever. But it is also possible that reading matter makes all the difference while room conditions have nothing to do with reading proficiency. A third possibility exists. There may very well be interaction between the two main effects, with the combination of one category of room condition and one category of reading matter producing a pronounced difference. If we had three categories of reading matter, entertaining fiction, technical material in a field the reader is an expert in, and technical material in a field new to the reader in addition to the three categories of room conditions, it might well be that the combination of technical material in an unknown field in a room under noisy conditions produces scores far lower than any other combination. A one way analysis would not detect this interaction. This sort of problem calls for a factorial design.

We are interested not in one, but in two experimental conditions, as well as in the possible interaction between them. In our example we would be interested in the following variances:

First main effect (room conditions)

Second main effect (reading matter)

Interaction

Residual ("within")

For each of the three experimental mean squares (the two main effects and the interaction) an F ratio is computed by dividing by the corresponding error variance. In the simple example we have chosen for demonstration purposes both experimental conditions were divided into three arbitrarily chosen categories. Since the categories were thus fixed by the researcher, this type of factorial design is usually referred to as a fixed model design. Other designs are possible, notably the random model where both conditions are divided into randomly chosen categories, or the mixed model where one condition is divided randomly, the other arbitrarily on the basis of some logical considerations. The nature of the factorial design determines the error term to use in the computation of the F ratio. In our simple example we have a fixed model design and we divide each of our experimental mean squares by the within groups mean square to obtain the desired F ratios. A summary table would list three F ratios as follows:

$$\frac{\text{Room condition MS}}{\text{Within groups MS}} = F \text{ for room condition effect}$$

$$\frac{\text{Reading matter MS}}{\text{Within groups MS}} = F \text{ for reading matter effect}$$

$$\frac{\text{Interaction MS}}{\text{Within groups MS}} = F \text{ for interaction effect}$$

We will not attempt to describe the computational steps for a two way analysis of variance here. Many detailed discussions of this topic have been published elsewhere. The reader is referred to the General Bibliography. But let us assume we had actually performed the analysis, probably with the help of a computer, and obtained the following results:

Source	SS	df	MS	F	Significance
room conditions	120	3	40	10.0	$p < .01$
reading matter	30	2	15	3.75	$p > .01$
interaction	18	6	3	.75	$p > .05$
residual	160	40	4		
total	328	51			

We would interpret all this to mean that, under a predetermined α level of .01, different room conditions did indeed lead to different reading proficiency scores, while no evidence exists that the other main effect or the interaction between both main effects have anything to do with the differences in reading scores.

APPENDICES

APPENDIX 1.

NOTES ON THE USE OF THE COMPUTER

The invention of the computer has opened many fields of human activities to quantitative research methods. Library science can profit from these developments. The prime factors that have prevented librarians in the past from exploiting the opportunities of data presentation, summarization, and analysis offered by statistical methodology were (1) the difficulty of reducing library phenomena to quantitative data, and (2) the enormity of the computational labor involved in such quantitative research. In the past, it was simply unfeasible to conduct even relatively unsophisticated descriptive studies, for example, if they involved hundreds of pairs or even triplets of numerical observations, no matter how much insight into the long term dynamics of library operations one could have gained thereby.

Consider the case of library collection size standards that have been developed in many branches of librarianship. Few if any studies have been conducted that would test these standards against actual achievements on a long range basis. In the junior college field, to pick a specific example, the ACRL standards for collection size are closely tied to enrollment. For every unit increase in enrollment, the standards specify, the library must acquire X units of books in addition to a minimum collection of Y volumes.

While it is easy enough for an accreditation team or a self-study group to compute the requisite number of volumes for a college library at one given time, it would involve considerable arithmetic work to compute a long range trend comparing enrollment with holdings in the historical perspective of the entire life of the institution. If one wished to expand such a study into a nationwide comparison, the cost in time and energy for the computational work involved would almost certainly outweigh the immediate benefits. Yet it would be most beneficial to have data of this kind, if only to obtain a base line against which to measure other proposals such as the California formula, a proposed standard that takes staff size, student body size, and number of subject fields taught into consideration. This standard, also called the Clapp-Jordan formula, is based on purely subjective decisions and not much is known about its practical value. The formula could be tested if it were applied retroactively to the body of national junior college library statistics accumulated over the last fifty years. One simple way to do this would be to construct a theoretical trend line, computed by means of a few well-known equations. This trend would show decisively whether librarians can gain something by the application of the Clapp-Jordan formula, or whether the old standards produce the same results in the long run. And all this is easy to do, but only if a computer can be pressed into service to do the computational work.

The reader can probably think of dozens of other projects that did not get done in the past because they were not feasible from a computational point of view. How can the computer help? There are two types of computer services, batch-mode and time-sharing. Batch-mode installations require that the data be prepared in some machine readable format, usually punched cards done to certain specifications. The punched input is turned over to an operator and the output becomes available to the researcher some time later.

Time-sharing systems in the sense in which we use the term here are computers that afford the researcher direct communication with the installation via a keyboard input console or terminal and a print-on-paper or cathode ray screen output display.

On both types of systems two routes are open to the investigator. He can use existing program libraries that are available on all major installations today, or he can write his own programs.

Program libraries offer a great variety of descriptive routines such as means, standard deviations, correlation coefficients, regression equations, trend lines, and many others. There is also an almost infinite variety of ready-made programs for chi square tests, t tests,

F-tests, and other aids to statistical analysis. Some of these programs
originate in the specific installation, they are home-made programs.
Others are acquired from outside sources, for example Univac's STAT PACK,
the University of California's BIOMED package, or the Funk and Scott
PREDICASTS TERMINAL SYSTEM (PTS). Most computer manufacturers offer
further ready-made statistical programs.

By way of an example, we shall present the key steps a researcher
must follow to use such a ready-made program on a time-sharing, terminal-
controlled installation. While the specific computer instructions of
our example will of course only work on one particular computer, in this
case a Hewlett-Packard System 2000E, its features serve well as a model
for other installations' instruction sets. They demonstrate the basic
principles of computer use that can be applied to other program libraries
and different computers. The program described here goes under the name
CORREL. Its purpose is to compute an r coefficient for any set of
bivariate data.

To use the program the investigator would begin by studying the
documentation available at the computer installation. In our case the
following guidelines have been published:

Program name: CORREL
Function: COMPUTES A CORRELATION COEFFICIENT
Data input: TYPE "9000 DATA N"
                 WHERE N IS THE NUMBER OF DATA PAIRS

                 TYPE "9001 DATA X,Y..."
                 WHERE X,Y ARE THE DATA PAIRS

After typing a prearranged user code into the terminal keyboard to activate
the system the investigator calls for the program by typing the following
command:

GET-$CORREL

The computer responds with a message:

CORREL IS READY

Suppose the investigator's research project called for a correlation between volumes at end of year and volumes added during the year, for the twenty-one public four-year college libraries in the State of New York.   The data are organized as follows:

	Volumes at end of year (X)	Volumes added (Y)
Library 1	97,648	5,390
Library 2	805,227	33,720
.	.	.
.	.	.
.	.	.
Library 21	X_{21}	Y_{21}

According to the guidelines given, the investigator types now the number of data pairs, in this case 21:

9000 DATA 21

Next, the data themselves:

9001 DATA 97648, 5390, 805227, 33720...

As soon as the twenty-one data pairs have been entered the investigator types the command

RUN

and the computer responds instantly with the result:

THE CORRELATION COEFFICIENT IS .519

The entire operation, assuming the investigator types accurately at moderate speed, takes less than three minutes. Compare that with the time it would take to compute r for these data by hand.

The only guidelines needed for using a batch-mode computer are detailed input format specifications. The user is not involved in any further decisions, commands, or instructions to the computer since the programs are handled by the operator. These ready-made programs are very valuable to the researcher, of course, but they have one drawback: each program can do only what is was written for. The researcher with a unique problem often finds that none of the programs in the installation's program library will do exactly what he wants done with data in the form inwhich he has them. In such cases a researcher is at a great advantage if he can write his own program.

The second way to utilize the computer in library research, therefore, involves original programming. This method recommends itself particularly for time-sharing terminal operations because of the directness of communication between machine and user. Let us demonstrate such a situation by means of the following fictitious example. Published national college library statistics often include a ratio of books per student. This ratio is the simple unweighted quotient of total holdings divided by total enrollment. Since this ratio is sensitive to both, holdings and enrollment, it is a very ambiguous measure of quality. Obviously, one way to increase the ratio is to increase the holdings. Clearly, 10,000 books for a student body of 1,000 yields a books per student ratio of 10. And 20,000 books for the same student body yield a higher ratio: 20. Yet there is another way to achieve the same high ratio, and that is a reduction of the student body size. Uncontestably, 10,000 books for a student body of 500 also yield a ratio of 20. Here are some fictitious data of this kind:

College	Enrollment(FTE)	Holdings	Books/FTE
A	1,000	11,000	11
B	2,000	10,000	5
C	2,500	12,000	4.8

We can see that in terms of Books per Full Time Equivalent enrollment (FTE) , College A is superior to Colleges B and C.
This, as we have seen, is unconvincing as a measure of library
quality.

Let us say a researcher wished to make a fresh start and
re-examine these statistics. For any given sample of colleges
at any given period of time the enrollment figures can be
determined. When ranked from lowest to highest, a median enrollment figure for the sample can be established. The median,
as we have shown earlier, is not sensitive to extreme score
values and does therefore serve well to summarize such a set
of fluctuating data. In the absence of better theory, our
researcher might select the median enrollment as a representative
average value. He can use this average as a convenient base line
with which to compare all his institutional data. He might re-
compute the Books per FTE ratios, this time not by the traditional
formula

$$\frac{\text{Holdings}}{\text{Enrollment}}$$

but by a new formula

$$\frac{\text{Holdings}}{\text{Median Enrollment}}$$

Here are the same fictitious data in their new dress:

College	Enrollment (FTE)	Holdings	Books per FTE (weighted)
A	1,000	11,000	5.5
B	2,000	10,000	5.0
C	2,500	12,000	6.0

We can see that, after adjustment for comparative enrollment size,
College A is no longer in the superior position in terms of Books
per Student. And this demotion is justified since the high unweighted
Books per Student ratio owed its magnitude to lack of students, not
excellence of library.

Suppose this is the problem facing a researcher. How would he use a computer to solve it? There is, of course, no program written that would compute the weighted books per student ratio for college libraries. He will have to write his own.

The elements of the art of writing computer programs in a common language such as BASIC or FORTRAN can be learned in a short time. Many educational institutions offer such instruction and all future librarians should enroll in at least one such course as part of their preparation for modern librarianship. We shall not attempt any instruction in the writing of computer statements, or "coding", in these pages. There are many excellent books available in this field.

Moreover, it should be kept in mind that such coding, the work that involves a knowledge of a computer language, is only a small fraction of the total intellectual task of writing a program for a statistical routine. By far the greater part of that task is the detailed effort it takes to understand the structure of the data involved and the logic that governs the planned analysis.

We can, therefore, without going into the details of coding, give some guidelines how to set up a research problem for computer programming. We shall do this by continuing with the example we started. We shall aim for a display, a tabulation, of enrollment data, library holdings, and the weighted Books to Student ratio. Let us assume the project involved 2,122 libraries included in Report OE-15023-69 of the United States National Center for Educational Statistics. The program to produce the desired display consists of three major parts as follows:

1. INPUT (and STORE)
   a. Identification code for each college (ID)
   b. Number of fulltime students, each ID
   c. Number of part time students, each ID
   d. Number of books in the library, each ID

2. COMPUTE (and STORE)

    a. Full Time Equivalent (FTE) for each ID

    b. Median enrollment for the distribution

    c. Weighted Books to Students ratio for each ID

3. PRINT OUT

    a. ID

    b. Number of full time students

    c. Number of part time students

    d. FTE enrollment

    e. Number of books in library

    f. Weighted Books to Students ratio

The example given is, of course, trivial and could be executed faster by hand using a pocket calculator. But that was not the point. What we do want to impress upon the reader is that only when the steps of a proposed project have been thought through and laid out carefully in a logical pattern can a programmer design an efficient program to process the data. And the beauty of that is that short shrift can be made of even the most voluminous and complex analyses in minutes or hours when it would take weeks or months if attempted with pencil and paper.

BASIC MATHEMATICAL CONCEPTS

In much of the statistical work done in the course of quantitative library research formulas play an important part. Formulas are generalized expressions of specific algebraic operations performed on variables. More often than not, formulas employ certain conventional symbols to designate units, variables, and operations.

In a set of data involving one variable, that variable is customarily referred to as X. If there is only one single variate, one observation, this is clear enough. The symbol X stands for that one observation. But usually we are interested in data that consist of many observations on a variable. We might have a set of collection size data, as follows:

UNIT	VOLUMES (X)
Library 1	30,000
Library 2	40,000
Library 3	35,000
Library 4	25,000

There is a variable X with four variates. To generalize such a tabulation one uses the following conventional symbols:

X: the variable, in this case VOLUMES

X_1: the variate corresponding to the first unit observed, in this case number of volumes in Library 1

n: the total number of observations, the last observation, in this case 4

Using these symbols, one can convert the table into generalized form:

System of observed units	X
Ss_1	X_1
Ss_2	X_2
$\vdots$	$\vdots$
Ss_n	X_n

The symbol Ss, of course, stands for "observed unit". If a second variable is involved the customary symbol for it is Y. We might have a data table like this:

System of observed units	X	Y
Ss_1	X_1	Y_1
Ss_2	X_2	Y_2
$\vdots$	$\vdots$	$\vdots$
Ss_n	X_n	Y_n

Occasionally, different variables are designated by subscripted X'es. This requires two subscripts for the variates, one for the row (horizontal dimension) and one for the column (vertical dimension). Here is a generalized table for n rows and k columns:

System	X_1	X_2	$\cdots\cdots$	X_k
Ss_1	X_{11}	X_{12}		X_{1k}
Ss_2	X_{21}	X_{22}		X_{2k}
				$\vdots$
Ss_n	X_{n1}	X_{n2}		X_{nk}

This tabulation is sometimes called an "n by k" table. The variate X_{21} is read "eks two one", or "eks sub two one", never "eks twenty-one".

The standard symbols for algebraic operations are familiar to most. Addition is symbolized by the sign +; subtraction by −; multiplication by ·, x, X, or∗ , or simply by juxtaposition of two or more variables and their numerical coefficients. Thus, the following operations are all equivalent:

$$2 \cdot b$$
$$2 \times b$$
$$2 \; X \; b$$
$$2 \ast b$$
$$2b$$

Division is symbolized by : or /. The following operations are equivalent:

$$12 : a$$
$$12 / a$$

$$\frac{12}{a}$$

The operation of raising a quantity to a higher power is indicated by a superscript to the right of that quantity, the exponent:

$$a^2 \qquad y^{1/2} \qquad m^n$$

The reverse operation, extraction of a root, is symbolized by the sign $\sqrt{}$:

$$\sqrt[2]{a} \qquad \sqrt[n]{k}$$

One other operational symbol is frequently encountered in statistical work, the summation sign, Σ :

$$\sum_{i=1}^{n} X_i$$

This means that we are to sum, add up, all the variates of the variable X, beginning with the first (i=1) and ending with the nth (i=n). The same instruction is sometimes simplified to read ΣX.

In the event of an n by k array of data of which the grand sum is to be taken, adding the variates over all rows and columns, two summation signs are needed to describe the operation:

$$\sum_{i=1}^{n} \sum_{j=1}^{k} X_{ij}$$

Here is a simple table on which these operations have been performed:

10	18
12	12
13	20
35 +	50 = 85

Statistical work requires a knowledge of elementary algebra. For reference and review we repeat a few of the more common principles. Algebraic operations are performed on numerical values (2,15,88) and numbers represented by letters, or literals (a,b,x). In this context, numerals are often referred to as constants and literals as variables.

Any group of variables and/or constants involving an algebraic operation such as addition or multiplication is referred to as an algebraic expression. The following are all algebraic expressions:

$$a + b$$
$$2ab$$
$$a + 3x \qquad \text{and} \qquad \frac{m}{\sqrt{9}}$$

The product or quotient of any two or more numbers, variables or constants, is called a term or a monomial. Thus, the following are terms:

$$2 \quad (i.e.\ 1 \cdot 2)$$
$$b \quad (i.e.\ 1 \cdot b)$$
$$2ab \qquad \text{and} \qquad \frac{m}{\sqrt{9}}$$

Two or more terms whose literal parts are exactly alike are called like terms or similar terms. These are like terms:

$$a$$
$$2a$$
$$\frac{3}{4}a$$

Terms differing in the literal parts are called unlike or dissimilar terms. Thses are unlike terms:

$$a$$
$$2x$$
$$\frac{3}{4}x^2$$

Any algebraic expression that contains more than one term joined by an addition or a subtraction sign is referred to as a polynomial. The following are polynomials:

$$c + d^2$$

$$a^2 + 2ab + b^2$$

$$8e + 12b - 6a + 21mn$$

The first polynomial in this example, $c + d^2$, is composed of only two terms. Such polynomials go under the special name of binomials.

Only like terms can be added or subtracted algebraically. Thus it is possible to perform the following addition:

$$\begin{array}{r} 4b \\ + 6b \\ \hline 10b \end{array}$$

However, one cannot add 4b and 6c since these are unlike terms. Likewise, it is possible to do this subtraction:

$$\begin{array}{r} 26x^2 \\ - 25x^2 \\ \hline x^2 \end{array}$$

But one cannot subtract 9y from $18y^2$.

Numbers and terms may be positive or negative. Unfortunately, convention forces us to use the symbols + and − for two different purposes. In the following example they are used to designate positive and negative values, respectively:

$$+2a$$

$$-3b$$

In the earlier example of a binomial, on the other hand, the symbol +
denoted the operation of addition:

$$c + d^2$$

For complete precision we should show this binomial in the following
form:

$$(+c) + (+d^2)$$

spoken "positive c plus positive d^2". In real life, however, this is
seldom done unless it is required for special emphasis. The sign is
always understood to be positive unless specifically stated otherwise.

To add two like terms with like signs one simple adds their
absolute values and gives to the sum the common sign. Here is an
example done two ways:

Showing signs	Conventional notation
$(+6ab)$	$6ab$
$+ (+12ab)$	$+ 12ab$
$(+18ab)$	$18ab$

Here is an example of addition with negative terms:

$$-12mn^2$$
$$+ (-3mn^2)$$
$$-15mn^2$$

We added the absolute values and prefixed the common sign to the sum.

To add two like terms with unlike signs one takes the difference
between their absolute values and prefixes the sign of the larger value.
Here is an example:

$$12mn^2$$
$$+ (-3mn^2)$$
$$9mn^2$$

Here is another example of addition:

$$-16ab$$
$$+ \quad 2ab$$
$$\overline{14ab}$$

Subtraction is technically a branch of addition. To subtract one term from another we first reverse the sign of the term to be subtracted, and then proceed to add the terms in the usual manner. Thus, to subtract 2ab from 10ab, we do this:

$$10ab + (-2ab) = 8ab$$

To subtract −16xz from 80xz, we do this:

$$80xz + (+16xz) = 96xz$$

In a similar way we subtract −16xz from −80xz by this operation:

$$-80xz + (+16xz) = -64xz$$

In the addition of polynomials we first rearrange the terms so that all like terms fall in the same column; and then add the columns in the usual way. The problem of adding (−6ab + 3cd −9e) to $(2a^2 + 3cd + e)$ is accomplished as follows:

$$-6ab + 3cd - 9e$$
$$\underline{2a^2 \qquad\quad + 3cd + \ e}$$
$$2a^2 - 6ab + 6cd - 8e$$

The subtraction of polynomials proceeds in an analogous fashion. Here is an example: subtract (3xy − 2ab) from $(8x^2 - 10xz + ab)$. First we arrange the expressions into columns of like terms:

$$ab + 8x^2 - 10xy$$
$$-2ab \qquad\quad + 3xy$$

Then we reverse the signs of the subtrahend:

$$ab + 8x^2 - 10xy$$
$$+2ab \qquad\quad - 3xy$$

Finally we perform addition:

$$ab + 8x^2 - 10xy$$
$$\underline{+2ab \qquad\quad - 3xy}$$
$$3ab + 8x^2 - 13xy$$

Often we want to treat an expression as a unit. A common set of grouping symbols are the parentheses. We might enclose the binomial $c + d^2$ in parentheses:

$$(c + d^2)$$

This tells the reader that the quantity $(c + d^2)$ is to be treated as one unit.

Occasionally we encounter one sign of grouping within another, as in this example

$$(x + (2 - b + f) + y)$$

The inner set of parentheses can be removed to obtain this equivalent polynomial:

$$(x + 2 - b + f + y)$$

However, in removing a set of inner parentheses preceded by a minus sign care must be taken. For all the operational symbols within the inner parentheses must be reversed before the parentheses can be removed. The following two examples are equivalent polynomials:

$$(x - (2 - b + f) + y)$$
$$(x - 2 + b - f + y)$$

The product of two terms with like signs is always positive. Thus, the following products are equivalent:

$$(+4a) \cdot (+2) = (-4a) \cdot (-2) = 8a$$

The product of two terms with unlike signs, on the other hand, is always negative. The following products are equivalent:

$$(+2x) \cdot (-15) = (-2x) \cdot (15) = -30x$$

Any number raise to the first power equals itself. The exponent of such a power is never written. Thus $d^1 = d$. Any number multiplied by itself is said to be raised to the second power. This is indicated by a superscript 2 on the right, the exponent:

$$d \cdot d = d^2$$

If two like numbers raised to different powers are multiplied, the exponent of the product equals the sum of the exponents of the factors. Thus:

$$x \cdot x^2 = x^{(1+2)} = x^3$$

If two unlike literals are multiplied, their product is indicated by juxtaposition:

$$k \cdot p^2 = kp^2$$

If two terms multiplied with each other consist of literals and numerical coefficients, the coefficients of the product will be equal to the absolute value of the product of the coefficients. Here is an example:

$$13a \cdot 2b = 26ab$$

The multiplication of polynomials is accomplished by multiplying each term of the multiplier by every term of the multiplicand, thus:

$$2 \cdot (3a + c) = (2 \cdot 3a) + (2c)$$
$$= 6a + 2c$$

This simple operation can take on the appearance of complexity when several polynomials with multiple literals and different coefficients are involved. Here is a example:

$$(2a^2 + 7a - 10x^2y^3)$$
$$\cdot (4a - 6)$$

Since we must multiply each term of one group with every term of the other group, we simplify our life if we proceed as follows. First, we write the two polynomials one over the other, thus:

$$2a^2 + 7a - 10x^2y^3$$
$$4a - 6$$

Second, we multiply the first group by the first term of the second group:

$$2a^2 + 7a - 10x^2y^3$$
$$\underline{4a}$$
$$8a^3 + 28a^2 - 40ax^2y^3$$

Third, we multiply the first group by the second term of the second group:

$$2a^2 + 7a - 10x^2y^3$$
$$\underline{-6}$$
$$-12a^2 - 42a + 60x^2y^3$$

And finally, we add all like terms of the partial products to obtain the result:

$$+28a^2 + 8a^3 - 40ax^2y^3$$
$$\underline{-42a \quad -12a^2 \qquad\qquad\qquad\qquad + 60x^2y^3}$$
$$-42a + 16a^2 + 8a^3 - 40ax^2y^3 + 60x^2y^3$$

To square a monomial consisting of literals and a numerical coefficient one squares the coefficinet and doubles the exponent of all literal terms, thus:

$$(6xy^2)^2 = 36x^2y^4$$

To take the square root of such a monomial one takes the square root of the coefficient and halves the exponent of each literal:

$$\sqrt{9ab^4} = 3a^{\frac{1}{2}}b^2$$

To square a binomial such as (x+y) one multiplies the two terms with each other, multiplies the product by 2, and adds to that product the squares of the two terms, thus:

$$(x+y)^2 = x^2 + 2xy + y^2$$

The division of two algebraic terms with like signs leads to a positive quotient, thus:

$$\frac{6x^2}{3x} = \frac{-6x^2}{-3x} = 2x$$

The division of two algebraic terms with unlike signs gives a negative quotient, thus:

$$\frac{6a^3}{-3a^2} = \frac{-6a^3}{3a^2} = -2a$$

The quotient of two powers of the same base equals the base raised to the power of the difference between the two exponents:

$$\frac{a^4}{a^2} = a^{4-2} = a^2$$

The quotient of two equal powers of the same base equals 1:

$$\frac{x^3}{x^3} = x^{3-3} = x^0 = 1$$

If the exponent in the denominator is greater than that in the numerator, the exponent of the quotient is a negative number:

$$\frac{y^2}{y^4} = y^{2-4} = y^{-2}$$

A base raised to a negative power is equal to the reciprocal of that base with a positive exponent of the same magnitude:

$$y^{-2} = \frac{1}{y^2}$$

As a corollary of this, any factor in a fraction can be moved to the opposite side by simply changing the sign of the exponent, thus:

$$\frac{4a^2b}{x^3y} = \frac{4a^2bx^{-3}}{y}$$

When the root of some power of a quantity is to be taken, the result is equal to that quantity with an exponent consisting of the original exponent of that quantity divided by the index of the root. Here is an example:

$$\sqrt{a} = \sqrt[2]{a^1} = a^{\frac{1}{2}}$$

The reverse of this operation occurs frequently when higher powers are involved. Here is an example:

$$4^{\frac{3}{2}} = \sqrt[2]{4^3} = \left(\sqrt[2]{4}\right)^3 = 2^3 = 8$$

In the solution of equations, three axioms are most helpful:

1. The equation is unchanged if the same quantity is added to or subtracted from both sides.

2. The equation is unchanged if both sides are multiplied or divided by the same quantity.

3. The equation is unchanged if both sides are raised to the same power, or if the same root is taken from both sides.

The following four equations are equivalent:

$$x - 6 = 2 \qquad\qquad 2(x - 6) = 4$$

$$\frac{x - 6}{3} = \frac{2}{3} \qquad\qquad (x - 6)^2 = 4$$

In the solution of simple equations the library researcher frequently uses tables of squares. In most tables it is easy to find the square for a whole number. When fractions are involved, one should be guided by this rule of thumb: if the decimal point in the tabled value for n is moved one place, the decimal place in the tabled square must be moved two places in the same direction:

n	n^2
97	9409
9.7	94.09
.97	.9409

Tables of square roots are worked in a similar way. Square roots of whole numbers are easily read out. The procedure for fractions is best understood when the following relationships are kept in mind :

$$\sqrt{100\,n} \;=\; 10\,\sqrt{n}$$

$$\sqrt{\frac{1}{10}\,n} \;=\; \frac{1}{10}\sqrt{10\,n}$$

$$\sqrt{\frac{1}{100}\,n} \;=\; \frac{1}{10}\sqrt{n}$$

$$\sqrt{\frac{1}{1000}\,n} \;=\; \frac{1}{100}\sqrt{10\,n}$$

Many tables give values for both, $\sqrt{n}$ and $\sqrt{10n}$. Here are some examples of square roots for fractions:

n	$\sqrt{n}$	$\sqrt{10n}$
147	12.124	38.340

$$\sqrt{14.7} \;=\; \sqrt{\frac{1}{10}\,n} \longrightarrow 3.834$$

$$\sqrt{1.47} \;=\; \sqrt{\frac{1}{100}\,n} \rightarrow 1.21$$

$$\sqrt{.147} \;=\; \sqrt{\frac{1}{1000}\,n} \longrightarrow .383$$

APPENDIX 3

COMMON SYMBOLS

Symbol	Meaning		Symbol	Meaning
$+$	Addition		z	Standard score
$-$	Subtraction		s	Standard deviation, sample
$* \times x \cdot$	Multiplication		σ	Standard deviation, population
$: /$	Division		σ^2	Variance
$=$	Equal to		Q_1	25th percentile
$<$	Less than		Mdn	Median, 50th percentile
$>$	Greater than		Q_3	75th percentile
$\neq$	Not equal to		r	Correlation coefficient (Pearson)
$\leq$	Equal to or less than		ρ	Correlation coefficient (Spearman)
$\geq$	Equal to or greater than		df	Degrees of freedom
$\sqrt{}$	Square root		F	F statistic
$\| \|$	Absolute value		t	Student's t statistic
$\sum$	Summation		χ^2	Chi square statistic
X	Raw score		H_1	Research hypothesis
x	Deviation score		H_0	Null hypothesis
f	Frequencies		α	Alpha (probability)
i	Interval size			
N	Population size			
$\bar{X}$	Mean of sample			
μ	Mean of population			

(189)

APPENDIX 4

GLOSSARY OF TECHNICAL TERMS

ALPHA ERROR: Rejecting a null hypothesis when in reality it should have been accepted

BETA ERROR: Accepting a null hypothesis when it should have been rejected.

CHI-SQUARE: Method of hypothesis testing for categorical data.

CLUSTER SAMPLE: Selection of clusters from a population as opposed to selection of single cases.

CONFIDENCE INTERVAL: An interval set up to determine the probability of the occurrence of an event in sampling statistics.

CONTINUOUS VARIABLE: A variable that can take any value within an interval on the scale of measurement.

CONTROL: Efforsts to neutralize contaminating variables.

DATA: Observations, plural of DATUM

DEGREES OF FREEDOM: The number of observations in a sample, less the number of restrictions placed on the observations.

DEPENDENT VARIABLE: Variable affected by a change in an INDEPENDENT variable, q.v.

DISCRETE VARIABLE: A variable that can take only finite numbers and no fractions.

DOCUMENTATION: In computer programming, written description of a program with instructions for users.

F RATIO: The quotient of variation between groups and variation within groups.

FREQUENCY POLYGON: A graph depicting plotted frequencies.

HISTOGRAM: A graph depicting frequencies in the form of rectangles.

INDEPENDENT VARIABLE: A variable which is manipulated to produce a effect on one or more dependent variables.

(190)

INTERVAL DATA: Data measured on an equal interval scale
     with arbitrary zero point.

MEAN: Arithmetic average.

MEDIAN: Midpoint of an array of rank ordered data, an
     average, the 50th percentile.

MODE: The frequence that occurs most often in a distribution,
     an average.

NOMINAL DATA: Observations made on basis of membership of
     an observed unit in a category. Also called categorical
     data.

NORMAL CURVE: Statistical model of a theoretical distribution
     of chance event.

NULL HYPOTHESIS: A hypothesis set up to be tested.

OGIVE: A plot of cumulative proportions of frequencies.

ONE-TAILED TEST: A hypothesis test that points in one
     direction, as opposed to the TWO-TAILED TEST, q.v.

ORDINAL DATA. Quatities that express rank order, not
     magnitude. Also called ranking data.

POPULATION: Totality of subjects studied. May range from
     1 to infinity.

RANDOM SAMPLE: Sampling technique that affords every unit
     an equal chance of being selected.

RANGE: A measure of disperson for ranking data.

RATIO DATA: Data measured on an equal interval scale with
     absolute zero point.

REGRESSION: Technique for predicting values of one variable
     from knowledge of another variable.

RELIABILITY: Consistency of measurements.

RESEARCH HYPOTHESIS: Researcher's hypothesis stating in
     positive terms the expected results.

SCIENTIFIC METHOD: Methodology which emphasises the testing
     of hypotheses by means of analysing data collected on
     the basis of a rigorous research design.

SIGNIFICANCE: A level of probability chosen to test a hypothesis.

SKEWNESS: Property of a distribution when frequencies tend to concentrate at one end.

STANDARD DEVIATION: Measure of dispersion for ratio and interval data.

STANDARD ERROR: Standard deviation of the theoretical distribution of a sample statistic.

STRATIFIED SAMPLE: Sampling method by which the population is divided into sub-groups before random selections are made.

SYSTEMATIC SAMPLE: Procedure for selecting units from a list at pre-determined intervals.

t TEST: A test for determining the significance of a difference between two small-sample statistics.

TWO-TAILED TEST: A hypothesis test that does not point in a specific direction.

VALIDITY: Degree to which observations show what they are meant to show.

VARIANCE: A measure of dispersion. Square of the STANDARD DEVIATION.

z TEST: A test for determining the significance of a difference between two large-sample statistics.

Squares and square roots for integers from 1 to 100

N	N^2	$\sqrt{N}$	N	N^2	$\sqrt{N}$	N	N^2	$\sqrt{N}$
1	1	1.000	35	1225	5.916	69	4761	8.306
2	4	1.414	36	1296	6.000	70	4900	8.366
3	9	1.732	37	1369	6.082	71	5041	8.426
4	16	2.000	38	1444	6.164	72	5184	8.485
5	25	2.236	39	1521	6.245	73	5329	8.544
6	36	2.449	40	1600	6.324	74	5476	8.602
7	49	2.645	41	1681	6.403	75	5625	8.660
8	64	2.828	42	1764	6.480	76	5776	8.717
9	81	3.000	43	1849	6.557	77	5929	8.774
10	100	3.162	44	1936	6.633	78	6084	8.831
11	121	3.316	45	2025	6.708	79	6241	8.888
12	144	3.464	46	2116	6.782	80	6400	8.944
13	169	3.605	47	2209	6.855	81	6561	9.000
14	196	3.741	48	2304	6.928	82	6724	9.055
15	225	3.872	49	2401	7.000	83	6889	9.110
16	256	4.000	50	2500	7.071	84	7056	9.165
17	289	4.123	51	2601	7.141	85	7225	9.219
18	324	4.242	52	2704	7.211	86	7396	9.273
19	361	4.358	53	2809	7.280	87	7569	9.327
20	400	4.472	54	2916	7.348	88	7744	9.380
21	441	4.582	55	3025	7.416	89	7921	9.433
22	484	4.690	56	3136	7.483	90	8100	9.486
23	529	4.795	57	3249	7.549	91	8281	9.549
24	576	4.898	58	3364	7.615	92	8464	9.591
25	625	5.000	59	3481	7.681	93	8649	9.643
26	676	5.099	60	3600	7.745	94	8836	9.695
27	729	5.196	61	3721	7.810	95	9025	9.746
28	784	5.291	62	3844	7.874	96	9216	9.797
29	841	5.385	63	3969	7.937	97	9409	9.848
30	900	5.477	64	4096	8.000	98	9604	9.899
31	961	5.567	65	4225	8.062	99	9801	10.000
32	1024	5.656	66	4356	8.124	100	10000	10.000
33	1089	5.744	67	4489	8.185			
34	1156	5.830	68	4624	8.246			

Table B

Squares and square roots for selected fractions from .001 to .9

N	N^2	$\sqrt{N}$
.001	.000001	.0316
.01	.0001	.1
.1	.01	.3162
.002	.000004	.0447
.02	.0004	.1414
.2	.04	.4472
.003	.000009	.0547
.03	.0009	.1732
.3	.09	.5477
.004	.000016	.0632
.04	.0016	.2
.4	.16	.6324
.005	.000025	.0707
.05	.0025	.2236
.5	.25	.7071
.006	.000036	.0774
.06	.0036	.2449
.6	.36	.7745
.007	.000049	.0836
.07	.0049	.2645
.7	.49	.8366
.008	.000064	.0894
.08	.0064	.2828
.8	.64	.8944
.009	.000081	.0948
.09	.0081	.3
.9	.81	.9486

(194)

Table C.

Normal curve model. The table gives the proportion of the area in the greater part under the curve (A) for z values from 0.00 to 3.00. To find the area in the smaller part under the curve (B) subtract the tabled value from 1.0.

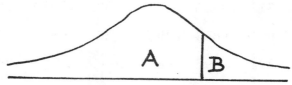

	0	1	2	3	4	5	6	7	8	9
0.0	.5000	.5040	.5080	.5120	.5160	.5200	.5239	.5279	.5318	.5358
0.1	.5398	.5437	.5477	.5517	.5556	.5596	.5635	.5674	.5714	.5753
0.2	.5792	.5831	.5870	.5909	.5948	.5987	.6025	.6064	.6102	.6140
0.3	.6179	.6217	.6255	.6292	.6330	.6368	.6405	.6443	.6480	.6517
0.4	.6554	.6590	.6627	.6664	.6700	.6736	.6772	.6808	.6843	.6879
0.5	.6914	.6949	.6984	.7019	.7954	.7088	.7122	.7156	.7190	.7224
0.6	.7257	.7290	.7323	.7356	.7389	.7421	.7453	.7485	.7517	.7549
0.7	.7580	.7611	.7642	.7673	.7703	.7733	.7763	.7823	.7852	.7881
0.8	.7910	.7938	.7967	.7995	.8023	.8051	.8078	.8105	.8132	.8159
0.9	.8185	.8212	.8238	.8263	.8289	.8314	.8339	.8364	.8389	.8413
1.0	.8425	.8437	.8461	.8484	.8508	.8531	.8554	.8576	.8599	.8521
1.1	.8643	.8664	.8686	.8707	.8728	.8749	.8769	.8789	.8809	.8829
1.2	.8849	.8868	.8887	.8906	.8925	.8943	.8961	.8979	.8997	.9014
1.3	.9031	.9049	.9065	.9082	.9098	.9114	.9130	.9146	.9162	.9177
1.4	.9192	.9207	.9221	.9236	.9250	.9264	.9278	.9292	.9306	.9318
1.5	.9331	.9344	.9357	.9369	.9382	.9394	.9406	.9417	.9429	.9440
1.6	.9452	.9463	.9473	.9484	.9494	.9505	.9515	.9525	.9535	.9544
1.7	.9554	.9563	.9572	.9581	.9590	.9599	.9607	.9616	.9624	.9632
1.8	.9640	.9648	.9656	.9663	.9671	.9678	.9685	.9692	.9699	.9706
1.9	.9712	.9719	.9725	.9731	.9738	.9744	.9750	.9755	.9761	.9767

Table C, continued

	0	1	2	3	4	5	6	7	8	9
2.0	.9772	.9777	.9783	.9788	.9793	.9798	.9803	.9807	.9812	.9816
2.1	.9812	.9825	.9829	.9834	.9838	.9842	.9846	.9849	.9853	.9857
2.2	.9860	.9864	.9867	.9871	.9874	.9877	.9880	.9883	.9886	.9889
2.3	.9892	.9895	.9898	.9900	.9903	.9906	.9908	.9911	.9913	.9915
2.4	.9918	.9920	.9922	.9924	.9926	.9928	.9930	.9932	.9934	.9936
2.5	.9937	.9939	.9941	.9942	.9944	.9946	.9947	.9949	.9950	.9952
2.6	.9953	.9954	.9956	.9957	.9958	.9959	.9960	.9962	.9963	.9964
2.7	.9965	.9966	.9967	.9968	.9969	.9970	.9971	.9972	.9972	.9973
2.8	.9974	.9975	.9976	.9976	.9977	.9978	.9978	.9979	.9980	.9980
2.9	.9981	.9981	.9982	.9983	.9983	.9984	.9984	.9985	.9985	.9986
3.00	.9986									

Table D

Critical values of t for two-tailed model:

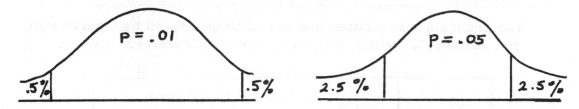

d.f.	p=.01	p=.05	d.f.	p=.01	p=.05
1	63.66	12.7	35	2.72	2.02
2	9.93	4.30	40	2.70	2.01
3	5.84	3.19	45	2.68	2.01
4	4.60	2.78	50	2.67	2.00
5	4.10	2.60	55	2.66	2.00
6	3.73	2.46	60	2.65	1.99
7	3.51	2.33	65	2.65	1.99
8	3.36	2.32	70	2.64	1.99
9	3.25	2.27	75	2.64	1.98
10	3.16	2.23	80	2.63	1.98
11	3.10	2.21	85	2.63	1.98
12	3.05	2.13	90	2.63	1.98
13	3.00	2.16	95	2.62	1.98
14	2.97	2.15	100	2.62	1,98
15	2.94	2.13	200	2.60	1.96
16	2.91	2.12	300	2.59	1.96
17	2.89	2.11	400	2.58	1.96
18	2.87	2.10	500	2.58	1.96
19	2.85	2.09	1000	2.58	1.96
20	2.84	2.09			
21	2.82	2.08			
22	2.81	2.08			
23	2.80	2.07			
24	2.79	2.06			
25	2.78	2.06			
26	2.77	2.05			
27	2.76	2.05			
28	2.76	2.05			
29	2.75	2.04			
30	2.74	2.04			

Table E

Chi-Square

The program was written and the table generated by George Roth and Jeffrey E. Sward, California State University, Fullerton.

	Value of Chi-Square	
d.f.	99% level	95% level
1	6.63	3.84
2	9.21	5.99
3	11.34	7.81
4	13.27	9.48
5	15.08	11.07
6	16.81	12.59
7	18.47	14.06
8	20.09	15.50
9	21.66	16.91
10	23.20	18.30
11	24.72	19.67
12	26.21	21.02
13	27.68	22.36
14	29.14	23.68
15	30.57	24.99
16	31.99	26.29
17	33.40	27.58
18	34.80	28.86
19	36.19	30.14
20	37.56	31.41
21	38.93	32.67
22	40.28	33.92
23	41.63	35.17
24	42.97	36.41
25	44.31	37.65
26	45.64	38.88
27	46.96	40.11
28	48.27	41.33
29	49.58	42.55
30	50.89	43.77

APPENDIX 6

SELECTED LIBRARY RESEARCH LITERATURE, ANNOTATED

Although there is much written on libraries and research, pertinent literature dealing specifically with the application of scientific methods and statistical techniques in the area of library science is negligible. Educators have been aware of this for a long time and the lack of comprehensive textbooks has made teaching in this field an extremely difficult task. Here, an attempt has been made to list the works that deal with library science research methods.

1. <u>Reader in research methods for librarianship.</u> Bundy, Mary Lee, Wasserman, Paul, and Araghi, Gayle, eds. (Washington, DC: NCR Microcard, 1970)

> The fundamental purpose of this volume of readings is to assist librarians to perceive the nature of scholarship and its relationship to the goals of librarianship. The articles -- mostly written by non-librarians -- emphasize the theoretical basis of social science research. Many of the selections are concerned with conceptual issues. One section of the volume is devoted to the presentation of illustrative conceptual formulations. The book is intended for individuals who are attempting to understand how research provided the capacity for a field to move forward.

2. <u>The scientific investigation of library problems.</u> Busha, Charles H., and Purcell, Royal (Proposal, ERIC ED 068 102)

> Plan for a graduate level textbook devoted to research methods. Objectives are as follows:
> a. provide complete presentation of the research process
> b. give adequate attention to quantitative aspects of data collecting
> c. emphasize theory and scientific rigor
> d. explain descriptive and inferential statistics
> e. balance design, measurement, and analysis
> f. facilitate isolation of productive areas of library research and generate appreciation of research
> g. stimulate students to question assumptions in library science

(199)

3. <u>Library operations research</u>. Daiute, Robert J., and Gorman, Kenneth A. (Dobbs Ferry, N.Y.: Oceana, 1974)

This is a report of a U.S. Office of Education -- funded research project on in-the-library book use, conducted at Rider College Library, Trenton, N.J. The report includes sections on sampling theory and computer methods employed in the analyses, including programs. Emphasis is on the details of the statistical analyses conducted during the study.

4. <u>An introduction to scientific research in librarianship</u>. Goldhor, Herbert (Urbana, IL: University of Illinois, 1968)

Result of author's experiences in teaching research methods. Typical topics discussed:
   a. logical design of a scientific research study
   b. scientific method
   c. role of theory
   d. hypotheses, causation, proof
   e. historical and survey research
   f. statistical analysis

5. <u>Research methods in librarianship: measurement and evaluation</u>. Goldhor, Herbert , ed. (Urbana, IL: University of Illinois, 1968)

Papers presented at a conference on measurement and evaluation held at the University in September 1967. Several of the papers written by librarians. All deal with aspects of measurement and evaluation, with emphasis on the nature of the relationships between people and books.

6. <u>Quantitative methods in librarianship: standards, research, management</u>. Hoadley, I. B., and Clark, A.S., eds. (Westport, CT: Greenwood, 1972)

Papers presented at an Institute held at Ohio State Univ. in August, 1968. Notwithstanding the title, this is not a treatise on methodology.

7. <u>The library school and research in librarianship in North America</u>. Lancour, Harold (Paper delivered to the Committee on Library Education, Council of the International Federation of Library Associations, 37th session, Liverpool, Sept. 1971)

General paper on the philosophy and principles of library research.

8. Introductory guide to research in librarianship and information science. Layzell, Ward Patricia (London: Polytechnic of North London, School of Librarianship, 1974)

   Helpful introduction into nature of research, for dissertation writers.

9. Basic statistics for librarians. Simpson, I. S. (Hamden, CT: Linnet, 1975)

   Essentials of statistics presented in a relatively simple form. An attempt to make statistics comprehensible to students of all backgrounds.

10. Research methods in librarianship: historical and bibliographical methods in library research. Stevens, Rolland E., ed. (Urbana, IL: Graduate School of Library Science, Univ. of Illinois, 1974)

    Papers from a conference dealing with historical research. Eight of the papers written by non-librarians, three by librarians.

11. Operations research: implications for librarians. Swanson, Don R., and Bookstein, Abraham, eds. (Chicago, IL: Univ. of Chicago, 1972.)

    Papers from the 35th Annual Conference of the Graduate Library School, Aug. 1971. Insights into the nature of the OR approach to libraries. A knowledge of mathematics is required to read this book.

12. Investigating library problems. Waples, Douglas. (Chicago: University of Chicago Press, 1939)

    A dated but scholarly essay on sound theory and logic in librarianship.

13. Research methods in library science: a bibliographical guide with topical outlines. Wynar, Bohdan S. (Littleton, CO: Libraries Unlimited, 1971)

    Bibliography of 800 annotated entries, with author and title index.

14. <u>Reader in operations research for libraries</u>. Brophy, P. and others (Washington, DC: NCR Microcard, 1976)

   Not available for review at time of this writing.

15. <u>Measuring the quality of library service: a handbook</u>. Beeler, M.C. (Metuchen, N.J.: Scarecrow, 1974)

   Attempts definition of total library service. Part I: survey of methods currently used to measure quality of library service. Part II: recommendations which are the result of research in library effectiveness. Part III: annotated bibliography dealing with measurement in library service.

16. <u>How to do library research</u>. Downs, Robert B. (Urbana, IL: University of Illinois, 1975)

   A book from another age. "Research" here means bibliographic searching.

APPENDIX 7

GENERAL BIBLIOGRAPHY

1. Arkin, Herbert and Colton, Raymond R. Statistical methods as
    applied to economics, business, psychology, education and
    biology. New York, Barnes and Noble (College Outline
    Series), 1966.

2. _____. Tables for statisticians. New York, Barnes and Noble
    (College Outline Series), 1963.

3. Averill, E. W. Elements of statistics. New York, John Wiley,
    1972.

4. Babbie, Earl E. Survey research methods. Belmont, CA, Wadsworth
    Publ. Co., 1973.

5. Barzun, Jacques and Graff, Henry F. The modern researcher. New
    York, Harcourt, Brace and World, 1957.

6. Bernstein, Allen L. A handbook of statistics solutions for the
    behavioural sciences. New York, Holt, Rinehart and Winston,
    1964.

7. Beveridge, William I. B. The art of scientific investigation.
    W.W. Norton, 1957.

8. Borg, Walter R. Educational research: an introduction. New York,
    David McKay, 1963.

9. Bundy, Mary Lee, Wasserman, Paul and Araghi, Gayle, eds. Reader
    in research methods for librarianship. Washington, DC, NCR
    Microcard, 1970.

10. Bunks, Barbara and others. A student's guide to conducting
    social science research. New York, Human Sciences Press, 1975.

11. Campbell, D.T. and Stanley, J.C. Experimental and quasiexperi-
    mental designs for research. Chicago, Rand McNally, 1963.

12. Champion, Dean J. Basic statistics for social science. Scranton
    PA, Chandler, 1970.

13. Cochran, W. G. Sampling techniques. 2d. ed. New York, John
    Wiley, 1963.

204

14. Converse, Jean M., and Schuman, Howard. Conversations at random:
     survey research as interviewers see it. New York, John Wiley,
     1974.

15. Cronbach, Lee J. Essentials of psychological testing. 3d. ed.
     New York, Harper and Row, 1970.

16. Davis, James A. Elementary survey analysis. Englewood Cliffs,
     NJ, Prentice-Hall, 1971.

17. Downs, Robert B. How to do library research? Urbana, IL, Uni-
     versity of Illinois, 1966.

18. Edwards, A. L. Experimental design in psychological research.
     3d ed. New York, Holt, Rinehart and Winston, 1968.

19. _____. Statistical analysis. Rev. ed. New York, Holt,
     Rinehart and Winston, 1968.

19.a Emory, C. William, Business research methods. Homewood, IL,
     Richard D. Irwin, 1976.

20. Ferguson, George A. Statistical analysis in psychology and
     education. 2nd ed. New York, McGraw-Hill, 1966.

21. Ferman, Gerald S. and Levin, Jack. Social science research:
     a handbook for students. Cambridge, MA, Schenkman Pub.
     Co., 1975.

22. Fowler, W. S. The development of scientific method. New York,
     Macmillan, 1962.

23. Galfo, Armand James. Interpreting educational research. 3d ed.
     Dubuque, IA, W, C. Brown Co., 1975.

24. Glazer, Myron. The research adventure: promise and problems of
     field work. New York, Random House, 1972.

25. Goldhor, Herbert. An introduction to scientific research in
     librarianship. Urbana, IL, University of Illinois, 1968.

26. _____. Research methods in librarianship: measurement and
     evaluation. (Papers presented at the Conference conducted by the
     University of Illinois, Graduate School of Library Science,
     September 10-13, 1967). Urbana, IL, University of Illinois,
     1968.

27. Gorden, Raymond. Interviewing: strategy, techniques and tactics. Homewood, IL, Dorsey, 1969.

28. Guilford, J. P. Fundamental statistics in psychology and education. New York, McGraw-Hill, 1965.

29. Hempel, Carl G. Philosophy of natural science. New York, Prentice-Hall, 1966.

30. Hoadley, I. B. and Clark, A.S., eds. Quantitative methods in librarianship: standards, research, management. (Proceedings and papers of an institute held at the Ohio State University, August 3-6, 1969). Westport, CT, Greenwood Press, 1972.

31. Holsti, Ole R. Content analysis for the social sciences and humanities. Reading, MA, Addison-Wesley, 1969.

32. Isaac, Stephen and Michael, William B. Handbook in research and evaluation for education and behavioural sciences. San Diego, Robert R. Knapp, 1974.

33. Kaplan, Abraham. The conduct of inquiry: methodology for behavioral science. San Francisco, Chandler Publ. Co., 1964.

34. Keppel, Geoffrey. Design and analysis: a researcher's handbook. Englewood Cliffs, NJ, Prentice-Hall, 1973.

35. Kerlinger, Fred N. Foundations of behavioural research. 2d ed. New York, Holt, Rinehart and Winston, 1973.

36. Koenkar, Robert H. Simplified statistics for students in education and psychology. Totowa, New Jersey, Littlefield, Adams, 1971.

37. Koosis, Donald J. Business statistics: teach yourself the quick proven way with programmed instruction. New York, John Wiley, 1968.

38. Lancour, Harold. The library school and research in librarianship in North America. (A paper delivered to the Committee on Library Education, Council of the International Federation of Library Associations, 37th session, Liverpool, England, September 2, 1971).

39. Lee, Robert. Research in librarianship: course outline and bibliography. Emporia, KS, Graduate Library School, Kansas State Teachers College, 1970.

206

40. Levin, Jack. Elementary statistics in social research. New York, Harper and Row, 1973.

41. Lohnes, Paul R. and Cooley, William W. Introduction to statistical procedures: with computer exercises. New York, John Wiley, 1968.

42. Longley-Cook, L. H. Statistical problems and how to solve them. (College Outline Series). New York, Barnes and Noble, 1968.

43. McInnis, Raymond G. and Scott, James. Social science research handbook. (College Outline Series). New York, Barnes and Noble, 1974.

44. Miller, Delbert C. Handbook of research design and social measurement. 2d ed. New York, McKay, 1970.

45. Millman, Jason, and Gowin D. Bob. Appraising educational research: a case study approach. Englewood Cliffs, NJ, Prentice-Hall, 1974.

46. Noether, Gottfried E. Introduction to statistics: fresh approach. New York, Houghton, Mifflin, 1964.

47. Oppenheim, A. N. Questionnaire design and attitude measurement. New York, Basic Books, 1966.

48. Ray, William S. An introduction to experimental design.

   New York, Macmillan, 1960 .

49. Rosen, Lawrence and West, Robert. A reader for research methods . New York, Random House, 1973.

50 . Ross, Robert. Research: an introduction. New York, Barnes and Noble, 1974.

51. Ruch, Floyd L. and others. Elementary statistics in psychology and education. Columbia, MO, Lucas Bros., 1957 .

52. Rudner, Richard S. Philosophy of social science. Englewood Cliffs, NJ, Prentice-Hall, 1966.

53. Schofield, George. Social research. London, Heinemann, 1969.

54. Siegel, Sidney . Non-parametric statistics for the behavioural sciences. New York, McGraw-Hill, 1956.

55. Simon, Julian L. Basic research methods in social science.
    New York, Random House, 1969.

56. Simpson, I.S. Basic statistics for librarians. Hamden, CT,
    Linnet Books, 1975.

57. Sjoberg, Gideon and Nett, Roger. A methodology for social
    research. New York, Harper and Row, 1968.

57.a Snedecor, George W., and Cochran, William G. Statistical methods.
    6th ed. Ames, Iowa, Iowa State University Press, 1967.

58. Spence, Janet T. and others. Elementary statistics. 2d ed.
    New Tork, Appleton-Century-Crofts, 1968.

59. Stevens, Rolland E. Research methods in librarianship:
    historical and bibliographical methods in library
    research. Urbana, IL Graduate School of Library Science,
    University of Illinois, 1974.

60. Stuart, Alan. Basic ideas of scientific sampling. New York,
    Hafner, 1962.

61. Suchman, Edward A. Evaluative research: principles and
    practices in public service and social action programs.
    New York, Russell Sage Foundation, 1967.

62. Taylor, Peter A. An introduction to statistical methods.
    Itasca, IL, Peacock, 1972.

63. Thorndike, Robert L. and Hagen, Elizabeth. Measurement
    and evaluation in psychology and education. 3d ed.
    New York, John Wiley, 1969.

64. Van Dalen, Deobald B. Understanding educational research.
    New York, McGraw-Hill, 1973.

65. Wandelt, Mabel. Guide for the beginning researcher. New
    York, Appleton-Century-Crofts, 1970.

66. Waples, Douglas. Investigating library problems. Chicago,
    University of Chicago Press, 1939.

67. Warwick, Donald P. The sample survey: theory and practice.
    New York, McGraw-Hill, 1975.

68. Webb, D. T. and others. Unobtrusive measures. Chicago,
    Rand McNally, 1966 .

208

69. Weiss, Robert E. Statistics in social research: and intro-
    duction. New York, John Wiley, 1968.

70. Wiersma, William. Research methods in education: an
    introduction. Philadelphia, Lippincott, 1969.

71. Williams, Frederick. Reasoning with statistics: simplified
    examples in communications research. New York, Holt, Rinehert
    and Winston, 1968.

72. Wilson, E. Bright Jr. An introduction to scientific research.
    New York, McGraw-Hill, 1952.

73. Wynar, Bohdan S. Research methods in library science: a
    bibliographical guide with topical outlines. Littleton, CO,
    Libraries Unlimited, 1971.

74. Young, Puline. Scientific social surveys and research: and
    introduction to the background, content, methods,
    principles, and analysis of social science. 4th ed.
    Englewood Cliffs, NJ, Prentice-Hall, 1966.

75. Zeisel, Hans. Say it with figures. 5th rev. ed. New
    York, Harper and Row, 1968.

76. Zwicky, F. and Wilson, A.G., eds. New methods of thought
    and procedure. New York, Springer-Verlag, 1967.

Exercise 1.

DATA 1. Number of entries for seven randomly chosen countries included in STATISTICS SOURCES, ed. by Paul Wasserman:

Country	Number of entries
Madagascar	27
Sudan	35
Uganda	50
Sweden	112
Haiti	33
Switzerland	84
Cyprus	55

For the data given above report the mean and the standard deviation.

$\overline{X}$: _____

s: _____

Exercise 2.

DATA 2. Prices of hard cover books in a random sample of 19 books taken from BOOK PUBLISHING RECORD for Feb. 1975.

Books(#)	US$	Books(#)	US$
1	26.50	11	8.95
2	8.95	12	13.00
3	20.95	13	37.50
4	19.95	14	18.00
5	16.95	15	21.95
6	5.00	16	17.95
7	14.95	17	5.50
8	8.95	18	40.00
9	18.00	19	7.00
10	5.95		

For the data given above compute these summary statistics:

Mean:_____

Median: _____

Standard deviation: _____

Exercise 3.

DATA 3. Public library expenditures in eight of the United States of America. Adapted from BOWKER ANNUAL for 1974.

State (coded)	Library $
1	490,280
2	176,090
3	274,070
4	176,480
5	3,918,780
6	993,550
7	893,720
8	148,090

For these data, compute these summary statistics:

$\overline{X}$ = $_____

Mdn = $_____

s = $_____

Exercise 4.

DATA 4. Two measures of ratio quality taken on each of eight subjects in a sample (fictitious data).

Subject #	X	Y	Subject #	X	Y
A	86	4	E	54	1
B	75	3	F	40	1
C	64	4	G	92	5
D	73	2	H	35	1

For these data, compute the r coefficient:_____

Exercise 5.

DATA 5. Population and library budgets for eight cities.
Adapted from BOWKER ANNUAL for 1974.

City	Inhabitants	Library $
A	869,600	4,017,580
B	752,250	3,078,000
C	641,930	4,335,850
D	735,000	2,890,210
E	549,490	1,643,380
F	405,000	1,560,420
G	925,000	5,886,550
H	357,000	1,084,860

For these data compute the rho coefficient and the
r coefficient.

rho: _____

r: _____

Exercise 6.

A strictly fictitious fairyland researcher believes that
a university's attractiveness for Ph.D. candidates rests at
least in part on the size of its library. To test this assumption
the researcher reasons that, everything else being equal, a
university with a large library should graduate more Ph.D.'s
in English and Journalism in a given year than a university
with a small library. Suitable data for nine comparable
institutions have been collected from published reports.
Fill in the missing blanks and answer the questions below.

University	X	Y	x	y	x^2	y^2	xy
1	4.4	4	−4.7	−2.3		5.4	11.1
2	10.6	8	1.4	1.7		2.8	2.4
3	10.2	6	1.0	−0.3		0.1	−o.3
4	22.0	6	12.8			0.1	
5	5.9	9	−3.3		10.7	7.1	
6	11.3	9			4.5		
7	10.2	6			1.1		
8	4.4	5		−1.3	22.7		6.3
9	3.6	4		−2.3	31.0		12.9
Sums:							
Means:							

What is the correlation coefficient r? _____

(a) How strong is the relationship between library size and number of Ph.D. graduates?

(b) What percentage of the variation in number of Ph.D. degrees awarded is explaine by variation in library size?

Exercise 7.

DATA 7. Circulation and gifts received per year, in eleven libraries.

Library	Per capita circ.	Gifts($)	Library	circ.	Gifts ($)
1	2.9	16,500	6	4.7	82,600
2	6.3	14,900	7	2.3	700
3	5	82,500	8	3.8	1,700
4	2.3	15,800	9	2.1	11,000
5	6.2	16,400	10	6.2	52,200
			11	7.1	47.300

Two library directors conclude that, when it comes to gifts and endowments, those who have, to them is given more. To test this, compute the correlation coefficient (r) for the data given above.

(a) Pearson's r: _____

(b) The two librarians decided that gifts, after all, have very little to do with per capita circulation. Are they justified in this conclusion, according to the data?

Exercise 8.

It was observed that in a sample of university libraries the total amount of money spent for books and periodicals appeared to be directly related to the total amount of private gifts received in a certain year. Here are the data:

DATA 8.

Annual income from private gifts (X) (1000$)	Annual total spent for books (Y) (1000$)
196	771
112	411
242	1896
319	907
33	52
428	1213
306	1525
183	1112
85	180

Compute the rho coefficient for these data _____

214

Exercise 9.

A cataloger believes that plain chronological subject headings subdivisions of the type

U.S.--HISTORY--1815-1848

are much easier to file than mixed alphabetico-chronological ones such as

U.S.--HISTORY--WAR OF 1812

He suspects that there is a relationship between the occurrence of mixed subdivisions in a catalog, and the number of mis-filed cards. To test this, he selects a sample of fifteen catalog drawers. For each drawer, the percentage of mixed subdivisions is established by the formula:

$$\frac{\left(T - Non\right) - P1}{Ts} * 100$$

where T is the total number of subject cards, Non stands for number of non-subdivided cards, P1 stands for the plain chronological subdivisions, and Ts for the total of sub-divided headings. For each drawer, the total of misfiled cards is recorded. Here are the data.

DATA 9.

Drawer#	Percentage mixed	Total misfiled	Drawer#	Percentage mixed	Total misfiled
1	51	3			
2	63	2			
3	83	24	9	39	8
4	77	9	10	22	6
5	80	11	11	36	15
6	37	4	12	54	16
7	85	17	13	13	1
8	92	18	14	14	5
			15	75	19

(a) compute rho coefficient: _____

(b) interpret. Is the cataloger's suspicion justified?

Exercise 10.

In a school library, frequency of class visits fluctuates from week to week. The number of students using the library on their own in the afternoon hours also fluctuates. It is suspected (hoped?) that there is a relationship between class visits and independent library use. A record is kept for some time. Here are the data.

DATA 10.

Week #	Number of class visits	Afternoon attendance
1	4	2
2	9	7
3	5	4
4	11	8
5	9	8
6	9	7
7	10	8
8	6	5
9	9	8
10	8	7

a. compute the r correlation: _____

b. what is the direction? _____

c. what is the strength of the relationship, in words?

EXERCISE 11.

DATA 11. A time series of fictitious data.

Year	Measurement
1967	64
1968	61
1969	70
1970	56
1971	87
1972	71
1973	91
1974	99
1975	95

Compute the linear regression coefficient, or slope (b): _____

Also compute a predicted measurement value for year 1980:

_____

EXERCISE 12.

DATA 12. Annual book production of a European country.
Data adapted from BOWKER ANNUAL for 1974.

Year	Titles
1961	24,890
1962	25,070
1963	26,202
1964	26,150
1965	26,350
1966	28,880
]967	29,610
1968	31,420
1969	32,390
1970	33,480
1971	32,530
1972	33,140
1973	35,250

Compute the linear coefficient b:_____

Predict the number of titles expected for 1980 (assuming
linear trend):

_____

EXERCISE 13

For DATA 4 (page 210), column X, compute the 95 per cent confidence interval.

CI_{95} lower limit: _____

     upper limit: _____

EXERCISE 14

For DATA 4 (page 210), column X, compute the 99 per cent confidence interval.

CI_{99} lower limit: _____

     upper limit: _____

EXERCISE 15

A sample of fifty books was taken from a batch waiting for recataloging. They were processed. The time taken to recatalog each book in the sample was recorded. The mean time taken was 35 minutes. The standard deviation was 12 minutes. At the 95 per cent confidence level, estimate the range within which the true mean time for the batch is likely to be found.

Lower limit: _____

Upper limit: _____

218

EXERCISE 16

A sample of 100 students was selected at random from
high school student body of 2,000. Their check out records
were examined for previous semester. The mean number of
check outs was 6 books per semester. The standard
deviation was 4 books. At the 95% level, estimate the
range within which the population is likely to be.

Lower limit: _____

Upper limit: _____

EXERCISE 17

A library employs outside help to catalog 2,000 books
per year. The charges vary according to difficulty.
to evaluate this service the librarian needs to find
the mean cost for thesee2,000 books. A sample of 50
is selected. The mean comes to $5.00. The standard
deviation is $4.00.

a. at 95% level, what is the probable population
   mean?

b. if the librarian can be certain at 99% level
   that the population mean is between $5.50
   and $6.50 she would continue the service.
   On the basis of the data, can you advise her
   to do so?

            yes   no

c. as the confidence level increases (from 95%
   to 99%), what happens to the confidence
   interval?

         it decreases

         it increases

         it stays the same

EXERCISE 18

A researcher wanted to know the average cost of a library's periodical subscriptions. He drew a sample of 100 subscriptions and found a mean cost of $13.20, with a standard deviation of $2.30.

What was the standard error of the mean?

———————

EXERCISE 19

DATA 19. Two samples of eleven shelf list cards were taken. They come from two different drawers chosen at random. For each book listed the size in number of pages was recorded.

Drawer BF

372, 444, 328, 158, 226, 627, 342, 106, 229, 436, 509

Drawer D

338, 322, 327, 149, 301, 183, 413, 38, 440, 339, 182

Compute the means for both samples and evaluate the difference.

$$t =$$

a. significant at 99% (α =.01)?

b. would you accept or reject the null hypothesis of no difference?

220

EXERCISE 20.

DATA 20. 99 male and 98 female librarians were rated on a scale of professional characteristics.

	Males	Females
Excellent	36	29
Good	33	33
Fair	18	20
poor	12	16
	99	98

For data 20 combine fair and poor into one category "bad". Compute the proportion of individuals rated bad in each of the two groups and determine the difference between the two proportions at the .01 level.

$$t =$$

a. difference significant?

b. do the data indicate that more women than men are rated bad?

EXERCISE 21

In a certain town the director of the public library would like to determine how the public feels about the library. A sample is taken of those townspeople who moved to the place as adults. This is Group I. Another sample is taken of those townspeople who were born there. This is Group II. The director suspects that the two groups differ in their attitude toward the library. To test this hypothesis he measures attitude with a standardized scale. Here are the data.

DATA 21. Summarized sample findings.

Group I	Group II
$\overline{X} = 28$	$\overline{X} = 20$
$s = 15$	$s = 12$
$N = 37$	$N = 37$

a. what is "t" for DATA 21? _____

b. what is the probability of a t this large
or larger having arisen by chance from a
population of equal means?   p _____

c. At the 99% level, do you accept or reject?

d. Would you say there is, or there is not
a difference?

EXERCISE 22

A library changed its fine structure and overdue
policies. Before the change a sample was taken of
1,000 circulation transactions. These were followed
up and note was taken of the number of transactions
that resulted in overdues. Sixty-five per cent were
returned in time, 35 per cent became overdue. After
the change, another sample of 1,000 transactions was
taken. The percentage of overdues was 28. At the
99% level, is the difference between the two samples
significant?

EXERCISE 23

An experiment to determine the durability of three types
of library glue resulted in the following scores (fictitious interval data):

Type I	Type II	Type III
62	77	72
58	79	69
68	73	70
64	83	65

By analysis of variance, compute F. Significant at .01 level?

EXERCISE 24

DATA 24. Number of days it took each of three vendors to deliver ten books chosen at random from those delivered during a given three month period. Data adapted from an article in Library Resources and Technical Services.

Vendor A	Vendor B	Vendor C
12	39	55
21	32	31
31	31	42
40	25	38
23	62	38
20	32	31
31	39	38
56	39	38
15	39	91
22	39	38

a. is F significant at .01?

b. would you accept or reject the null hypothesis of no difference in mean delivery times between vendors?

ANSWERS TO EXERCISES 1 - 24.
==

1. Mean = 57; standard deviation = 29

2. Mean =$16.63; Median = $16.95; s = $9.74

3. Mean = $883,882; Median = $382,175; s = $1,187,550

4. r = .86

5. rho = .86; r = .87

6. r = .28;(a)weak;(b) 8%

7.(a) r = .45; (b) yes, only ten percent explained.

8. rho = .77

9.(a) rho = .69; (b) yes

10.(a) r = .95; (b) positive; (c) strong

11. b = 4.9; 1980 prediction: 121

12. b = 1295; 1980 prediction: 44,659

13. Lower limit: 47.7; upper limit: 82

14. Lower limit; 44.5; upper limit: 85.25

15. Lower limit: 31.65; upper limit: 38.35

16. Lower limit: 5.22; upper limit: 6.78

17. (a) lower limit: 4.88; upper limit: 6.12; (b) yes; (c) increases

18. $s\bar{X}$ = .23

19. t = 1.13; (a) not significant; (b) accept

20. t = -.96; (a) not significant; (b) no

21. t = 2.5; (b) p > .01;(c) accept; (d) no difference

22. significant

23. significant

24. (a) not significant; (b) accept.